Emily Chalmers

with words by Ali Hanan

cheap chic

affordable ideas for a relaxed home

RYLAND
PETERS
& SMALL
LONDON NEW YORK

photography by Debi Treloar

First published in the United Kingdom
in 2003 by Ryland Peters & Small
Kirkman House
12–14 Whitfield Street
London W1T 2RP
www.rylandpeters.com

10 9 8 7 6 5 4 3 2

ISBN 1 84172 473 4

A CIP record for this book
is available from
the British Library.

Printed and bound
in China.

Senior designer Catherine Griffin
Senior editor Henrietta Heald
Location research Claire Hector,
  Emily Chalmers
Production Patricia Harrington
Art director Gabriella Le Grazie
Publishing director Alison Starling
Stylist Emily Chalmers

contents

THIS PICTURE Colour and pattern contrasts are used to add pizzazz to this dining room. With 'rhapsody in blue' as the main theme, bright, bold patterns have been juxtaposed to give the room life and soul. Floor cushions do the same job as furniture – at half the price. In the background, a garland of floral fairy lights introduces a festive touch.

LEFT AND BELOW LEFT Cheap chic involves thinking laterally about everyday objects. Here, handy handbags have become stylish storage for a little girl's bedroom, and a blue feather trim adds a touch of Africana to a simple lamp found at a car-boot sale.

RIGHT Reclaim, recycle, reinvent. When hand-picking things for your home, don't ignore retired items, which in a new setting can become objects of desire. These simple French-style milk, coffee and water jugs are on the shelf and loving it.

introduction

Cheap Chic will help you to create interior chic on the cheap. Packed with imaginative ideas, this book is a bible for the budget-conscious who also strive for style. Money, after all, can't buy good taste. Style is instinctive – and it can come at a snip as long as you have an eye for beauty as well as a bargain. As the interiors doyenne Andrée Putman once put it, '[To have] style is to see beauty in modest things.'

To the owners of the homes illustrated in this book, vision is more important than cash. From a retro-style terraced house in London to a modern rustic home in Amsterdam, each interior has been selected for its savvy style. As you look at these pages, be inspired by the way the owners have ingeniously cherry-picked the things they live with to shape well-designed homes that don't need a designer label.

What makes cheap chic so desirable is how easy it is to achieve. There are numerous shortcuts. From faking it to making it, there are countless ways to create a to-die-for interior at prices that won't make your heart stop. By scrimping in some areas, you can dine out in others. Spend your hard-earned cash on low-cost necessities and save a little extra for an investment buy – that single beautiful object or a floor that will last a lifetime.

LEFT **As it evolves over the years, a home becomes a living diary of the people who have dwelt in it and made their mark on the place. This engaging dog-on-wheels, for example – once a child's much loved toy – is a witty memento.** RIGHT **In this wooden housescape, nature's own highlights – a bowl of fruit and red roses in former liqueur bottles – give the room a visual kick.**

'Each one of these interiors has been so carefully considered,' explains *Cheap Chic*'s stylist and researcher, Emily Chalmers. 'To get luxury for less, you must be patient. Things don't turn up overnight. Be choosy and spend wisely.' View objects laterally. Work magic. Innovate. Wave your style wand and turn a smooth door into a table-for-six. Who cares if it's not the real thing? Fake it. Veneer floors, for example, make fabulous forgeries.

What all the owners recommend is to start with what you've got. Before you renovate, begin the budget-friendly way by working with what you inherit. Peel back carpets, scuff off wallpapers and hot-wash faded curtains. Reclaim vintage fabrics, original floorboards and rustic-style brickwork. A fresh hand-sewn sofa cover or a wash of bright new paint costs next to nothing, apart from a little time and effort.

That's what you need to get style on a shoestring. While the high street has good-value pieces, high-street looks are ubiquitous. Avoid the humdrum. Mix eras and styles by looking in less predictable places. For purse-friendly panache, follow your bargain-hunting instincts. Set your style sights on ethnic shops, junk stores, flea markets, jumble sales, auctions, architectural salvage yards, building sites, even pavement throw-aways – the list is endless.

For chic that's cheap, take inspiration from the interiors shown in this book. You will soon discover that you don't need to be wealthy to have a wealth of style.

THIS PICTURE Tailor's models show off wooden plumber's beads, necklaces of dried chillies and garish garlands of green crystal. They make a dramatic display in the hallway of this old house, where the floor has been brought back to life by a simple lick of paint.
OPPOSITE, BELOW RIGHT This simple table has both decorative and practical uses. It makes a pedestal for two large handsome vases and provides storage space beneath for a collection of trainers.

the elements

colour and pattern

Nothing changes a room as quickly as colour. What's more, it is so easy to do. All it takes is a dash of blue or green or a splash of pattern. You can transform a room in an evening with a coat of paint, or inject vibrancy with a striking cushion. And, even better, the materials you use won't make your wallet see red.

Colour schemes not only influence mood, but you can use them – at low cost – to improve the whole shape and feel of a room. Remember the decorator's rule of thumb: light colours expand a space, while dark colours reduce it. In a small room, use pale colours to make it appear larger or create a den with dark colours. Another optical illusion is to make ceilings seem higher by painting the bottom half of a room a darker colour up to chest height and adding a lighter colour up to the ceiling. Or, if you have an oddly shaped room, flatten it out visually with monochrome colours. By using colour you won't have to spend your cash on an architect – bargain!

To choose a scheme, think of things that you love. Are you inflamed by the deep aqua blues, razor-sharp whites and fresh greens of Morocco? Or are you passionate about a particular era? Each

OPPOSITE Sky-blue walls make a perfect background in this house of sunny contrasts. Every object displayed on the dresser, from the turquoise bowls to the raspberry-pink packaging, adds a shot of colour.

THIS PAGE Geometric tiled floors, hot pink walls and a blue rubber covering on the stairs create a mélange of colour and pattern. The owner has made a feature of a coat rack, injecting dashes of aquamarine and orange into the entrance hall. To avoid visual overload, she has opted for a neutral white metal storage cabinet.

Give dull-looking objects a makeover by adding a show-stopping cover. From cushions to ironing boards, everyday items simply need a new wrap.

decade has had its own colour and pattern palette. In the 1950s, pastels and florals reigned supreme; in the 1960s, brash colours (hot pinks, scarlet reds and purples) and swirls dominated the mix; the 1970s loved geometrics and earthy colours; the 1980s splashed out on extravagant colour schemes and gold-leaf fleur-de-lys; while the 1990s was all neutrals and textural patterns.

In the 21st century, you can choose any of these – and then add your own spin. Mix and match from different eras at low cost. Paint your walls in 1950s pastels – think baby pink, soft blue or quiet green – and add contrasts with big square floor cushions or curtains sewn from vintage or reproduction retro fabrics to create pockets of pattern. Or buy geometric 1970s wallpaper in the colours of the decade – bright orange, earthy brown and pea green – and contrast the pattern with a plain brown leather sofa.

OPPOSITE **While the overall scheme in this child's bedroom is restful, the circular, candy-striped cushion on the bed and the shelf accessories introduce eye-catching contrasts.**

ABOVE LEFT **Injecting a little pattern pizzazz, these cheerful wallflowers become outstanding features of an otherwise utilitarian kitchen.**

ABOVE CENTRE **Blue coat hangers have been teamed with a pink shirt against a door coloured in soft lemon. The yellow provides the canvas, while the aqua blue and pink make the still-life painting on top of it.**

ABOVE **A rolltop bath looks drop-dead gorgeous in pastel pink against a white wall. Although paint is often used to spruce up walls, it can add swathes of colour to a room and highlight pieces such as this tub.**

LEFT **One way to introduce bright hues without changing one iota of your interior is by taking advantage of nature's own colour show: flowers. These pink roses displayed in delicate Moroccan tea glasses represent a simple, stunning example of flower power.** BELOW LEFT **Era-ureka! Chinoiserie cushion fabrics meet swinging 1970s wallpaper. A mix of eras and styles in this Dutch house creates an eye-stopping interior. To find similar wallpapers, look for vintage prints in the bins of second-hand shops or new wallpaper swatchbooks. With the recent wallpaper revival, many companies are doing fabulous reprints of hip hits.** THIS PICTURE **Out-of-sight becomes sight friendly. Chests, cupboards and drawers in funky colours can be used to conceal all sorts of clutter and eyesores. By lowering the ceiling, these London homeowners have created ample storage space behind sliding cherry-red doors.** RIGHT **One wide taupe horizontal stripe brings a brushstroke of modernity to this neutral dining room.**

Whereas the 1990s was a whitewash of neutral colours and white, white paint, one of the trends to emerge in the first decade of the new century is the revival of wallpaper – and, with it, pattern. Trawl second-hand shops, which hoard rolls of vintage papers, or hunt through the latest catalogues for the nouveau ethnic designs – chinoiserie styles, African designs, modern florals – that are rolling off the presses and onto walls.

For a quick, low-cost update, give your walls a fresh coat of white paint – two coats of brilliant white will do – for that minimalist feel, and then paper just a single wall.

ABOVE **Colour and texture work like yin and yang. In this kitchen, ruddy tiles make a crossword-style backdrop for sombre Provençal-style cooking pots.**
ABOVE RIGHT **Far from a featureless passageway, this would-be wallflower of a stairwell is the belle of the house with its sunny-yellow 1970s wallpaper.**
OPPOSITE, LEFT **Instead of organizing your books alphabetically by author in the style of a library, order them according to height and colour and turn them into eye-catching features.**
OPPOSITE, RIGHT **A ruby-red bead curtain delineates space and brings in a splash of warmth. In front of it, an oriental floral paper lightshade, bought for a song, brings in a sky-blue contrast.**

If you discover a busy pattern or want to paint a stencil, don't overdo it. The trick is to think about highlights and contrasts. Combine patterns and plains to get the right balance. Add different tones for interest and bring these to life with contrasts. For example, blue blends well with green but is given a visual kick with a touch of orange; brown and taupe make harmonious partners, but the partnership can be spiced up with turquoise and mustard yellows.

The key to getting the overall scheme right is good planning. To make the process easier, use a stylist's trick and create a swatch book. Cut samples or take Polaroids of the fabric, carpets or curtains you are intending to buy, then visit a hardware store to find

Combine subtly different shades of colour for interest, and bring these to life with contrasts.

the paint to match. If you are using paint, you can save yourself time and money by purchasing testers. Paint a large metre square of wall space in your chosen test shade and observe how the colour looks at different times of the day as the light in the room changes.

While colour and pattern live on in paint and fabrics, don't forget about accessories. One particularly eye-catching trick (look at *Elle Decoration* magazine) is to display accessories by hanging them. For a shot of pattern, pick your favourite dress, shirt or skirt and suspend it from a colourful coathanger over a wall or door. This would work equally well with the rest of your wardrobe. Hang out your handbags or string up your necklaces from nails or hooks.

OPPOSITE ABOVE, LEFT AND RIGHT **All good canvases are neutral. In a room with soft blue walls the eye is automatically drawn towards the sculptural fireplace and the curvaceous silhouettes of painted wooden chairs; the shelves are a stage for the sculptural forms of teapots, cups, saucers and mugs.**
OPPOSITE BELOW, LEFT **An ingenious way to bring in colour is to display your glorious garments. Hang them for highlights and for ideas. For example, the babygro inspired the stunning colour combination shown in the picture on this page.**
OPPOSITE BELOW, RIGHT **Floors, doors, walls and furniture – indeed, virtually any hard surfaces – are suitable for painting.**
RIGHT **Horizontal slats of colour revive the otherwise plain walls in this child's bedroom.**

Remember nature, which has some of the best colour and textures available. Buy big, colourful, long-stemmed flowers and put them centre-stage in any room for a huge shot of colour. Instead of traditional vases, improvise with cheap containers such as plastic buckets, wine coolers and bottles. For long-lasting looks, plant bulbs in teacups or breakfast bowls on a sunny window-ledge or buy flowering pot plants. Make your own fresh, floral garlands – simply buy carnations or other flower heads, thread them onto a long, colourful string and dangle them around your home.

Don't be reluctant to experiment. And, if you get bored with a particular colour or the look you want doesn't seem to be working in the way you intended, colour is easy to change with a flick of a paintbrush. Pattern works in a similar way. For a new feel, simply introduce different cushion covers, bedspreads, throws or rugs. A plain backdrop allows you to be fickle. Change from geometric to paisley or from paisley to floral. Create.

top tips for colour and pattern

MAKE THE MOST OF WHAT'S THERE For earthy tones, strip back surfaces. Underneath you may find original brickwork, floorboards or old flagstones, which cost nothing to you but look priceless.

GO NEUTRAL AND NATURAL The cheapest schemes often use the colours of raw materials – such as wooden floors and whitewashed walls – as a canvas; with a neutral backdrop, patterns and colours can come and go as you please.

TREAT YOUR INTERIOR LIKE YOUR WARDROBE Spend on accessorizing colours and patterns as you would on your own clothes; a new cushion or a swathe of vintage cloth often costs half the price of pair of shoes.

USE COLOUR TO ENHANCE ARCHITECTURE Rather than spending thousands taking down walls, renovating windows and lowering ceilings, use colour to create visual effects and maximize the potential of a room.

BE INSPIRED As interior doyenne Andrée Putman says, 'I have no recipe for how to combine things. But you must be sincere. And if you are, strangely, it will succeed.' In other words, don't follow convention. Mix patterns and colours that work for you.

fabrics

Soften a hard edge. Provide texture and colour, warmth and comfort. Partition a room. Gently filter light. Is there anything fabrics can't do? Even better, there are many fabrics that can be picked up for a snip.

As with most other things in the home, when it comes to fabrics it pays to invest in quality. Usually, this means natural fibres. For example, it is a false economy to buy cheap tea towels made of a polyester and cotton mix, which inevitably shrink. Instead, save your cash for second-hand linen tea towels. Why? Linen is an incredible fibre. Moisture-resistant, soft and strong – three times as strong when wet – it is the perfect material for tea towels, napkins, tablecloths and sheets.

Wool, too, outstrips its synthetic imitators. It can be bent up to 30,000 times without being damaged, making it ideal for floor rugs and sofa throws. Acting as a natural insulator, wool also preserves heat and soaks up noise. For inexpensive rugs, exercise your bartering skills at Persian shops or markets, or buy sheepskins and blankets from high-street stores.

One important feature of natural fibres is that they 'breathe' – which, when it comes to bed linen, helps the body to regulate its temperature. If you can't find second-hand linen sheets, try new

OPPOSITE, ABOVE AND BELOW LEFT **Fabrics that cost next to nothing can look a million dollars. For example, a piece of fur casually tossed over an old Turkish cushion makes a glamorous feature, and a ruddy felt basket provides smart storage for scarves.**

OPPOSITE, ABOVE RIGHT **A thick curtain, linen on one side and felt on the other, is suspended by a sturdy rod running through eyelets.**

OPPOSITE, BELOW RIGHT **Liven up an old tea towel or rejuvenate a blanket with a trim. The great thing about fabrics is that they allow you to ad lib. Sew on buttons, sequins, ribbons, beads or shells to make a Cinderella cushion the belle of the hall.**

THIS PAGE **Disguise an old sofa in style. Here, the sofa has been dressed up, softened with a dust sheet and highlighted with mix-'n'-match striped cushions.**

THIS PAGE **From the little notebooks propped up on a windowsill, all wearing flower-print dustcovers, to the soft cotton bag hanging from a doorknob, florals give these interiors a fresh, pretty look. Piles of fabrics, like piles of books, make a fabulous feature. It pays to choose natural fabrics because these endure more wear and tear than synthetic fabrics, as any antique linen tea towel attests.**

THIS PAGE **Combined and contrasted with contemporary pieces, the floral cushions and vinyl-coated tablecloth give these interiors a modern country feel. Rather than being fusty, florals, when set against clean white backgrounds, look fresh and soft. The fabulous thing about fabrics is you can change them with the seasons, as long as the canvas remains neutral, as here. This flowery look is an ideal style for spring.**

Egyptian cotton sheets, considered to be the best quality (at the best price). Rough-weave fabrics such as earthy hessian, horsehair and hemp not only breathe but also let the light through. For chic room dividers or window covers, buy these pieces as strips or panels from haberdashery stores.

Natural fabrics, unless dyed, have a limited colour range: stone, cream, chocolate brown, taupe, which is fine for a mother-earth palette. For a little rock 'n' roll, scour second-hand shops for off-beat fabrics – vintage bedspreads, dresses, jeans and coats – at rock-bottom prices. All you need is a little bit of imagination and a sewing machine. With scissors and thread, you can transform these pieces into floor cushions, sofa covers, curtains or patchwork blankets.

Keep your eyes peeled for classics such as faded florals, tweeds, cool corduroys and stone-washed denims. You are bound to find fabric friends to match your style. Retro lovers will search out vintage fabrics from the 1950s, 1960s and 1970s; soft modernists will favour faded florals and denims; traditionalists will covet tweeds; and those who love exoticana must seek anything from Indonesian batiks to Chinese silks and West African prints.

Ethnic shops are ideal hunting grounds for funky fabrics such as hot-pink, gold-rimmed Indian saris and Samoan tapa cloth that do so much to spice up an interior. A sari, for example, could become a vibrant table runner or a beautiful wall hanging; to transform a sari into a gauzy curtain, simply sew over an edge and thread onto a rail – when the breeze catches it, the fabric will billow and sigh.

Otherwise, recycle what you've got. A cheap way to make soft-to-cuddle cushions is to hot-wash your old jerseys to make felt, and sew them into

ABOVE **An exotic pattern meets subtle stripes in this arresting display of cushions. As such a bold combination illustrates, fabrics don't necessarily have to match to work together. The rule of thumb in fashion is to put everything into the melting pot of your own taste – and have the courage of your convictions.**
ABOVE RIGHT **Fabrics also make instant accessories, as shown by these cotton cloths draped casually over knobs on a kitchen cupboard to resemble scarves.**
RIGHT **The key to achieving true style on a budget is to keep your eyes open for materials in their natural habitats – think of your grandmother's collection of curtains, shawls and bedspreads – then recycle and adapt them with trimmings such as sequins and feathers, which can be used to add texture and colour.**

THIS PICTURE **Ethnic fabrics such as this beautiful bright sari and the chinoiserie-style cushion covers recall lavish cultures and exotic lands. Search out examples of global style in street markets and ethnic stores, or collect swathes of textiles during your overseas travels. Think laterally about their uses: a sari could make an exotic, ethereal window cover as well as a cheap-'n'-chic child's bedcover.**

top tips for fabrics

LET NATURAL FIBRES RULE Synthetic fabrics often lack the resilience of natural fibres. Favour wool, linen, cotton, silks and other long-lasting fibres, which are breathable, durable and sensuous.

BE INNOVATIVE Don't confine fabrics to bedrooms. Use swathes of heavy rough-weave fabrics as room dividers; hang long dyed-muslin panels over windows instead of curtains; stretch a striped canvas around a lampshade frame.

LOOK IN ODD PLACES Fabulous fabrics may have unlikely origins – your grandmother's shawls or your latest cast-offs, for example. Trawl second-hand shops for old curtains, dresses, tweed jackets and sew them into – well, anything!

CHANGE WITH THE SEASONS Dress your home with different textures and fabrics to reflect the time of year: fake fur and wool for winter; muslin and cottons for summer.

MATCH THE DURABLE AND THE DECORATIVE Making floor cushions? Use a sturdy fabric such as denim or suede for a backing and a cotton floral pattern for the front.

LEFT **A cheap, chic way to add warmth and comfort to your home, fabrics can cost nothing but ingenuity to find while creating a homely X factor.**
OPPOSITE, ABOVE LEFT **The best fabrics are rarely found in bolts. It takes time, a sharp eye and lateral thinking to find good cuts. Here stacks of Indian sari fabrics sit elegantly on a chair.**
OPPOSITE, ABOVE RIGHT **Beds are obvious fabric magnets. Thick, warm blankets come in all sorts of textures, from cashmere to mohair. For sheets, use only natural fabrics, such as this light floral cotton.**
OPPOSITE, BELOW LEFT **Find a photographic reprint service that does commissioned reproductions of your most-loved moments on cotton fabrics.**
OPPOSITE, BELOW RIGHT **Velvet cushions sit like jewels on this sofa. Warm to touch and long-lasting, velvet is lovely to linger over.**

covers. You can change an old sheet into a stylish tablecloth by the simple application of a colourful dye. Or try the reverse: turn a lace tablecloth into a bedcover or use as a window covering to diffuse sunrays into cobweb-like patterns. Don't forget that fabrics can also revitalize lacklustre bathrooms. Instead of buying dull white bath towels from high-street stores, use colourful beach towels to inject a little dash into your bathroom.

Fabrics are your home's clothes, and, like your own wardrobe, they can change with the seasons. Cushion covers, throws, sheets and blankets can come and go with the weather. Create a warm, curl-up atmosphere in your living room each winter with fake fur throws, hessian blinds and second-hand checked woollen blankets. As spring comes, pack them away – it's time for floral patchwork cushions, light muslin curtains and denim throws. Fabric is fantastically flexible. No other material used in the home does so much for so little.

window treatments

Treat yourself to a window treatment – and make it beautiful. Windows are a room's best asset. Harness the power of light using economical curtains, blinds, shutters and screens. Depending on the season and your need for privacy, there are plenty of shoestring solutions to covering windows with style.

If you need privacy without loss of light, choose light-diffusing window covers. Homemade covers are kind to wallets. For example, take an old roller blind and puncture it with rows of holes to let the rays dapple through. Or create a play of diffused light and colour with dyed muslin strips. First, buy three lengths of muslin (or similar fabric) to match the height of your window and tidy up the seams. Dye two of the strips a rust red and one a burnt orange. Using contrasting ribbon, tie them to screw-in hooks and hang them with the orange strip in the middle.

Fabrics such as muslin, voile, organdie or old lace, or Japanese blinds, are gentle on the purse. If you want a private space only at certain times of day, try using old-fashioned screens, which double as room dividers. Another solution, which combines diffusion with total blackout, are blinds and shutters, now available at reasonable prices

THIS PAGE AND RIGHT Opaque coverings such as muslins, voiles, silks and lace diffuse the light while shielding interiors from intrusive gazes. It is easy to find cheap lengths of these fabrics in haberdashery stores, but don't forget that you can reclaim and reuse old sheets, lace shawls and former tablecloths. A bobble trim adds an edge.

RIGHT, INSETS It's curtains for expensive curtains. For a neat finish, simply use yacht hooks bought from a chandlery and string up an army tent fabric to a metal wire (left); or use traditional curtain eyes and sling them along a painted broomstick, wire or mop handle (right). The curtain in the right inset is a mixture of linen for looks and wool for warmth.

Nothing beats a natural wash of bright sunlight on bare walls, fading from a sharp white to rose pink as twilight comes.

THIS PICTURE **A length of sari fabric with a rhythmic pattern diffuses a beautiful dappled light. Former bedspreads, wall hangings, scarves, vintage quilts and sequined saris make equally luxurious light filters.**

OPPOSITE, LEFT **Instead of shopping at traditional places for blinds, explore alternative sources such as ethnic stores. From Japanese rice-paper blinds to this Middle Eastern slatted-cane roll-up blind, you could find cheap covers at prices to light up your life.**

OPPOSITE, BELOW RIGHT **Horizontal slats of lights diffused through a white aluminium blind make a room seem wider, while vertical slats would make a ceiling appear higher. Venetian blinds allow illumination varying from total blackout to diffused light.**

OPPOSITE, SMALL PICTURE, LEFT **An old blanket hangs at the window in this stairwell.**

OPPOSITE, SMALL PICTURE, RIGHT **This window cover is elegantly strung out along an old piece of pipe (a length of scaffolding pipe would also do) by means of fabric loops. Such loops are easy to sew, but curtains like this can be found for a song at high street stores.**

LEFT A pleated cotton blind allows light a look in but disappoints prying eyes. Plants in an outside window box also provide a discreet screen.
BELOW LEFT Who needs blinds when you could replace them with strings of beads, artificial flower heads or mother-of-pearl circles like these?
THIS PICTURE Among the stylish alternatives to traditional blinds are low-cost pleated papers.

RIGHT One straightforward way to create a window screen is to use nature's own sun-swallowing blinds: long-stemmed flowers, tall houseplants or climbers. Arrange vases of flowers such as tiger lilies, tall roses and geraniums on a windowsill or create a swirly verdant cover with thick ivy or fragrant jasmine. A windowsill is the perfect site for plants that love sun, including herbs such as bushy basil and willowy mint.

from high-street stores. At night these give total blackout, but by day they can create architectural illusions: blinds allow horizontal slashes of light to enter a room, making it expand, while shutters let in vertical strips, making the ceiling appear higher.

For draught-free winter cosiness or for rooms penetrated by the glare of streetlights, total exclusion of light is desirable. You don't need budget-busting velvet curtains to achieve this. Instead, use thick, chunky alternatives such as old bedspreads, blankets, strips of denim, squares of felt, suede, an old rug attached to a wire with bulldog clips or vintage quilts strung up with ribbon. If you want absolute darkness, sew blackout fabric, available from most haberdashers, on to the window side.

There is one final option, which costs nothing: use no covering at all. Go for the 'Emperor's New Clothes' and leave windows as the architectural kings that they are. Nothing beats a natural wash of bright sunlight, fading from a sharp white to a rose-coloured light on bare walls as twilight comes. Stained-glass windows are often better left uncovered, too, since these create their own equally dramatic play of light while providing privacy. After all, windows are often the most striking feature in a room, so why hide them?

top tips for window treatments

RECYCLE Re-use or buy old shawls, bedspreads, rugs and blankets. Tie them onto screw-in hooks or sew the top section over a disused broomstick or curtain pole, and tie back with ribbon or rope.

MAKE YOUR OWN Non-fray fabrics do away with the need for a sewing machine. Alternatively, show off your loose ends by gently fraying away an inch or two. Use lengths of sari to fit long windows; buy suede skins, cut into squares, and tack them together; or string up antique lace tablecloths.

THINK SECOND-HAND Curtains often turn up at jumble sales and second-hand shops. You may spot a pair that simply need dry cleaning.

HAVE A FLUTTER ON A SHUTTER Architectural salvage yards are a good source of wooden shutters and blinds. Sand and repaint them before fitting.

SHOP AT ETHNIC STORES Eastern cultures have their own ways of treating light: Japanese rice-paper blinds blend in with minimalist interiors; Chinese folding screens, either painted or made from silk fabric, make a beautiful addition to any interior.

furniture

Stylish, functional, affordable: pieces of furniture can be all these and more. From inflatable plastic sofas to customized flat-pack stools, you need to sharpen your instincts for a bargain. Items can be freestanding (ideal for urban nomads) or tailor-made and built-in (perfect for people who are firmly settled) but neither need cost you dear.

When it comes to furniture, it pays to acquire a few key items that have been chosen for their quality, particularly a proper bed – after all, we spend a third of our lives asleep. If you buy a good bed now, you won't have to change it for at least ten years.

Investment buys should always be freestanding. Once you have put your money where your comfort is and bought, for example, an ultra-soft armchair, the piece can become your living companion, moving with you from place to place.

Another asset is a decent leather sofa, which, if it is a classic, will actually increase in value over the years and end up outliving you. Vintage leather sofas and chairs such as 1930s club armchairs perfectly illustrate the value of quality. As long as they are classic pieces and manufactured from good, strong – usually natural – materials, they will last and last. Strong, wipeable, polish-it-up leather (even white leather) is also one of the few sofa coverings that age with grace.

ABOVE A medicine cabinet of the type frequently found in hospital dispensaries fits into this stylish bathroom like a hand in a glove.

ABOVE LEFT This curvaceous, low-slung sofa provides a neutral background for covers, cushions and throws. These accessories can come and go to satisfy the owner's mood or the changing seasons. A piece like this is an investment.

LEFT If you are not fortunate enough to inherit beautiful objects like those that make up this 'still-life in furniture', track down your own from second-hand shops, architectural salvage stores and junk yards.

THIS PAGE **In this peaceful bedroom, white walls, ceiling and floor make a blank canvas for the bed-as-sculpture. A floral patchwork quilt softens the industrial-style frame, while two matching lamps flank the bed in stark contrast to the reclaimed side cabinets.**

Architectural salvage
yards and junk shops
often have old pieces
that need no more than
love, attention and
a coat of paint.

OPPOSITE PAGE **Items from different eras have been combined to add interest to this contemporary London house; here a 1970s brown-glass ashtray sits beside a 1950s Draylon lounge suite. Stylish retro armchairs and low coffee tables in good condition like these can often be found in second-hand furniture shops.**
THIS PICTURE **An old pair of curvy second-hand chairs has been recovered for a modern dining room. Re-upholstering or sewing new covers – think canvas, towelling or hessian for a hard-wearing material – is a low-cost way to give furniture a new lease of life.**

THIS PICTURE **Against a contemporary white canvas, old pieces such as a large refectory table have been resurrected. A former church pew provides seating, while in the background weather-beaten wooden sleepers make rustic-style shelving.**

OPPOSITE, ABOVE RIGHT **This chair is as famous as it is ubiquitous. An early example of bent plywood, it was designed at the start of the 20th century by Michael Thonet. By 1930, 50 million chairs had been produced – and the chair is still being manufactured today.**

OPPOSITE, BELOW, LEFT TO RIGHT **Cheap chic places to perch include a plastic child's chair with an African-inspired design, an old straw-seated stool revived by a lick of white paint, and a metal workstool softened by a striped cushion.**

If you don't have much spare cash, give serious thought to second-hand furniture, which usually scrubs up well. For example, it is easy (and relatively cheap) to give second-hand fabric-covered sofas a new lease of life by having them re-upholstered. Choose a hard-wearing fabric such as a striped canvas. Or, if the sofa is in good shape, simply sew a couple of coloured covers to fit, changing them when the mood takes you – or as small sticky hands or food and drink spillages add their own overtures to the orchestra of cover colours.

Unless you own your own home, avoid built-in furniture, which you won't be able to take with you when you move. If you do have a home of your own, the good news is that shelves, wardrobes and cupboards can be built without wallet-shattering consequences. Built-in storage is often the only way to finish the jigsaw of an oddly shaped room. Get a carpenter to install cut-to-fit shelves, cupboards or built-in seating with low-cost medium-density fibreboard (MDF) or rustic recycled wood. What makes a piece of furniture stylish is often in the eye of the beholder – or what it's teamed with. If your built-in cupboard lacks chic, jazz it up with sleek streamlined aluminium handles or pretty tear-drop plastic doorknobs.

When shopping for furniture, look anywhere and everywhere. A good place to start is the high street. For a Pop feel, go for fun items such as the mod-looking inflatable pieces found in all sorts

top tips for furniture

THINK INVESTMENT BUYS For your own comfort and sanity, invest in a few key portable pieces such as a decent, decadent bed and a sink-into sofa. When you move on, these pieces can go with you.

SHOP ON THE HIGH STREET Interior stores stock a range of styles that are already chic, such as retro reproduction pieces, or adaptable (don't judge a sofa by its cover – as long as it's a good solid style, you can disguise it with a new cover or throw).

LOOK OUT FOR THE UNEXPECTED Next time you are in your local Chinatown or Arabic enclave, look out for ethnic pieces. An oriental paper lampshade or an Arabic coffee table adds an exotic dash.

DON'T DISMISS TAILOR-MADE Built-in furniture does not have to be expensive as long as it is made from economical materials such as MDF. Add a thick coat of paint and accessorize.

BE RESOURCEFUL Trawl junk shops and car-boot sales, keeping your eyes open for general pieces that you can adopt and adapt.

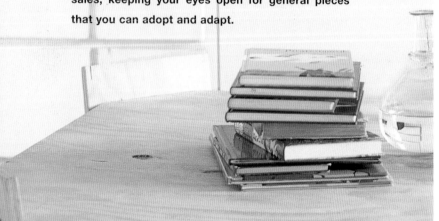

LEFT **Before splashing out on large pieces of furniture, think laterally and consider whether there might be a cheaper alternative. Many high-street stores offer low-cost pine dining tables, which you can customize with a lick of paint, stain or polish. Otherwise, adopt. Consider old desks, workbenches or former refectory tables. The most cost-effective solution is to build your own, as this ingenious owner has.**

of style stores. Mainstream interior stores also have great retro designs at purse-friendly prices. Look out for Robin Day plastic bucket seats and Verner Panton rugs, for example.

Then there is style beyond the high street. Ethnic furniture shops are full of treasures awaiting discovery, including Moroccan leather poufs, woven African footstools and in-laid mother-of-pearl Chinese side tables.

Architectural salvage yards and junk shops often have old pieces that just need a little love and attention and a coat of paint. The adage 'one person's trash is another person's treasure' also holds true – have a look in skips and examine pavement cast-offs.

Otherwise, be inventive and construct your own furniture. For example, rustic stools can be made from old tree trunks picked up in a salvage yard. Strip off the bark, sand the wood, stain, varnish and – *voila!* Or make a dining table by perching an old door on two trestles and covering it with a white linen tablecloth. Nail old railway sleepers together to make a rustic coffee table; use former wine boxes as shelves; put velvet cushions on wooden crates to make living-room stools. The key to embellishing your home with cheap chic furniture is lateral thinking.

THIS PICTURE Antique pieces such as this leather-clad
club chair from the 1930s are an investment. Leather
ages with grace, keeping its looks from decade to
decade. If you find an old piece that you love, hold
on to it because it may appreciate with time.
RIGHT AND BELOW RIGHT Try the high street for
contemporary stylish items on the cheap such as this
glass table top and the space-saving nest of tables.

storage and display

Space is one of your home's most prized possessions. When you free it up, you realize how much room you really have. Whatever your budget, the secret to good storage is to create a place for everything and put everything back where it belongs. It takes no more than a little ingenuity for all your belongings to find a home – and with style.

Good storage comes in many shapes and sizes and calls for many degrees of access. It's up to you to judge what to display. Bury old school books deep in an attic or under a stairwell, but keep aesthetically pleasing objects out in the open.

One of the cheapest – and easiest – ways to create storage space is to go Zen, throwing away all the junk in your possession and keeping only beautiful or useful things. Be ruthless: if you haven't worn an item for the past year, donate it to someone who will wear it. Swap books for cash or exchange old CDs. This process should make your storage problem seem much less of a mountain. As you finish filing your possessions, keep out the pieces that mean most to you. The rest can remain discreetly tucked away in cupboards and on shelves. With your possessions pared back to a minimum, you know that what you still own is what you really love.

ABOVE In a former life, these practical trolleys, now piled high with soft fresh towels and bedding, were used for transporting items around a factory.
ABOVE LEFT This galvanized-steel storage system is equally at home outdoors and in.
LEFT Old wooden filing drawers have been given a new lease of life as storage for odds and ends.
OPPOSITE A bank of cupboards makes the most of limited storage space in this pint-sized London apartment, enabling the owners to stash most of their possessions, including the television, neatly out of sight. Painted in a variety of neutral tones, the cupboard doors blend harmoniously with one another.

There are two main types of storage: built-in and movable. If you are an urban nomad, make movable storage one of your investment buys – think antique suitcases and vintage wooden tea chests. Such pieces often last for years, transporting precious belongings from home to home, and perhaps doubling as furniture when you settle. It's an old tradition: from the 17th century, when families emigrated to new worlds, all-purpose chests would be used to contain their entire belongings – and, after the destination had been reached, would double as beds or dining tables.

Movable storage means flexible storage, and it can also mean stylish storage. For example, a stack of old briefcases in cracked leather, a knot of red-lacquered Chinese jewellery boxes and a painted bookshelf turned into a home-office photo gallery can become show-stopping features in their own right. Build your own

ABOVE A capacious old medicine cabinet blends in with the sanitary feel of this contemporary bathroom. Storage pieces intended for public places such as restaurants, retail outlets, hospitals and libraries can often work equally well in domestic spaces.

TOP Mobile shelves fastened to a metal grid make flexible storage for spices and essential sundries. This kind of shelving – which allows everything to be kept in clear view – is ideal in a kitchen, where tasks often need to be carried out at speed.

ABOVE LEFT Sculptural stainless-steel pots, pans and kitchen utensils line up elegantly, swinging off butchers' hooks.

OPPOSITE A factory trolley makes a handy home for pairs of shoes. With this kind of storage, you can easily see what you've got and where it is at a glance – which makes it much simpler to be well organized.

THIS PICTURE This enormous storage cabinet doesn't quite reach the ceiling. A cupboard designed in this way deceives the eye into perceiving the room as more spacious than it is.

LEFT A rack of beautiful trays and dishes adds colour, texture and form to a kitchen. Blending practicality and aesthetics, this storage solution shows off objects that should not hide behind closed doors.

RIGHT If you have matching sets of plates, and cups and saucers, display them on open shelves.

BELOW RIGHT To exploit every inch of kitchen space, delicate teacups have been hung out of harm's way on wall hooks, adding a sculptural element to the room.

for next to nothing. For rough-edged industrial chic, mount a wooden plank on stacks of bricks. All these solutions look good and house your precious booty, but can move on when you do.

Built-in storage – an early-19th-century invention – may not be transportable, but it can be made to look superbly stylish at little expense. Use your DIY skills to construct cupboards and shelves or employ a carpenter to make these pieces out of low-cost materials such as medium-density fibreboard (MDF) and recycled woods. Many high-street stores have flat-pack off-the-peg units – shelves, drawers, cabinets – at affordable prices.

The great thing about built-in storage is that you can blend it seamlessly with your interior. For example, a floor-to-ceiling cupboard occupying an entire wall is a great way to create a huge storage space. Either make a feature of it, as shown on page 45, or paint it in a colour to match the rest of your room and use sturdy push-click fittings so that the cupboard unit looks just like part of the room (see page 49).

Built-in storage can make the most of the 'dead' spaces found in oddly shaped rooms – if you have a triangular alcove, you could square it off by putting in a corner cupboard or make a feature of it with shelves. Such storage can also be multipurpose. In your living room, for example, you could install built-in seating along one wall and put a hinged cover on the top to create storage underneath for videos, CDs and books.

When you sift through your possessions there will always be a special knot of items that cry out

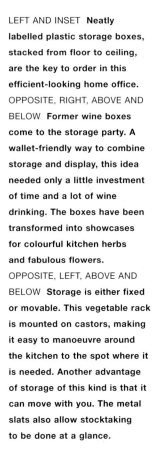

LEFT AND INSET **Neatly labelled plastic storage boxes, stacked from floor to ceiling, are the key to order in this efficient-looking home office.** OPPOSITE, RIGHT, ABOVE AND BELOW **Former wine boxes come to the storage party. A wallet-friendly way to combine storage and display, this idea needed only a little investment of time and a lot of wine drinking. The boxes have been transformed into showcases for colourful kitchen herbs and fabulous flowers.** OPPOSITE, LEFT, ABOVE AND BELOW **Storage is either fixed or movable. This vegetable rack is mounted on castors, making it easy to manoeuvre around the kitchen to the spot where it is needed. Another advantage of storage of this kind is that it can move with you. The metal slats also allow stocktaking to be done at a glance.**

The secret of good storage is to create a place for everything and put everything in its place.

to be displayed. Whether they are personal mementoes, such as photographs of loved ones, or collections of favourite objects, these are your own treasures and should be paraded with panache. To make them showstoppers, avoid convention and predictability. Rather than arranging your photographs on a mantelpiece in time-honoured fashion, clip them to a string and hang it along a hallway wall – or transform a stairwell or a cloakroom wall into a 'hall of fame' and put up large black-and-white portraits of your nearest and dearest.

Display your gorgeous things in disused or alternative spaces: stack books and magazines along a hallway instead of in fusty bookcases; dot flowers in Moroccan glass tea cups up the stairs; hang your Noel Coward-style dressing gown in the living room.

Instead of simply perching pieces on ledges, be original about how you present them. One way to economize on space and flaunt

THIS PICTURE Arranged along this industrial-style record storage unit is a mixture of shapes, colours and objects. Here, simple display has become a gallery of beautiful things, each one basking in its own glory.

OPPOSITE, LEFT If you own beautiful clothes, don't hide them. Make a feature of your robes, as this owner has. And, of course, if you hang your glad rags on a pole, you won't need to pay for a wardrobe to put them in, leaving more to spend on the clothes themselves.

OPPOSITE, CENTRE Far from their natural home on the floor, these wooden shoe-shapers make elegant hooks for bags in another storage-and-display double act.

OPPOSITE, RIGHT A magazine rack goes to the wall. This café-style newspaper and magazine tidy saves precious floor space.

OPPOSITE, ABOVE LEFT **Children's clothes need to be easily accessible. What better way to create cheap, stylish storage than to suspend them from a taut wire? Underneath, capacious storage boxes, bought for a song from the high street, house other essentials.**
OPPOSITE, BELOW LEFT **Home to winter coats, wellingtons, umbrellas and other fair-and-foul weather essentials, the hall is your home's hello. This one has been made welcoming with rustic storage solutions. Coats and bags hang from redundant driftwood, while scarves hide in a flaxen shopping basket.**
OPPOSITE, RIGHT **Old wooden apple crates, stacked atop one another, make rustic-style open shelving.**
RIGHT **Make a feature of your trainers by hanging them from basic metal hooks.**

your beautiful things is to hang them. All sorts of functional – and aesthetic – pieces look stunning when strung from racks, hooks or rails. Collections of copper pots and pans hung from butchers' hooks in a kitchen bring together practicality and artistry. Other ways to create eye-catching features include suspending utensils from rails and dangling tea cups from wall hooks.

In a bedroom, clothes don't always have to be locked away behind closed doors. An open clothes rail, for example, is a quietly simple way to make a feature of your clothes collection. Handbags, scarves, belts and evening bags draped from hooks nailed to walls not only make a stunning display but are also very easy to access.

Display the things you love, but give them room to breathe. Remember, a clutch of exquisite small stones collected on a seashore spree looks more arresting on an otherwise bare shelf than lost amid a crowd of other bits 'n' bobs. A small cluster is more effective than a load of clutter.

top tips for storage and display

REINVENT, RECYCLE AND REUSE Some ordinary household items offer great storage solutions. Jam jars and plastic ice-cream boxes, for example, make good air-tight food containers, while old doctors' bags and toolboxes make alternative containers for toiletries, sewing kits, scarves, gloves and hats.

'CREATE' SPACE In place of a wall, install a floor-to-ceiling storage system, accessible from both sides, built out of MDF. Or square off a corner with a triangular cupboard or shelf rack and 'create' space.

MAKE A FEATURE OF STORAGE Get hold of simple cardboard boxes or former fruit crates or shoeboxes and customize them with paint or stylish wrapping paper, or cover with vintage wallpaper.

OPT FOR ALTERNATIVE MATERIALS Clothes don't need to be housed in a wardrobe. Instead hang them off a clothes rail, using colourful paper shopping bags for underwear, T-shirts and sweatshirts.

DISPLAY YOUR WARES Don't keep your beauties behind closed doors. Mix open and closed shelving and put your Sunday best on display.

accessories

As the architect Mies van der Rohe once said, 'God is in the details.' This insight reflects one of the pillars of cheap chic interior style: make the most of accessories. On one hand, they are a home's personal signature – a visual diary of who you are and what you love. On the other, they are the practical objects that you couldn't live without.

Accessories usually fall into two camps: functional items such as crockery, utensils, cutlery, teapots and vases, and objects that are intended purely for decoration such as a child's finger-painting, a pristine shell found on a beach or a dried posy of red roses from a former lover.

Functional doesn't have to mean boring. The trick is to combine chic looks with usefulness. If you are buying brand-new cutlery, for example, high-street stores often have solid stainless-steel sets at reasonable prices. Find a set that the store intends to keep in stock and spread the cost by buying a few pieces every week. Most shops stock cheap-'n'-cheerful plastic cutlery sets, which are perfect garnish for Pop-style interiors. For the real thing – silverware – you can snap up a bargain by ferreting for heirloom sets or buying individual pieces, such as bone-handled knives, from second-hand markets, sales of antiques and junk shops.

THIS PICTURE Accessories don't have to match. Moroccan tea glasses, second-hand crockery, former biscuit tins and plastic tumblers mix like old friends socializing at a party. Cluster items together in this way but don't clutter. Give everything room to breathe.

OPPOSITE, TOP Cheerful candy-coloured plastic cups and a pea-green lemon squeezer are just part of a set of mismatched objects that introduce colour, funk and form to this display.

OPPOSITE, MIDDLE An enamel milk jug makes a convenient teaspoon tidy. Plastic-handled cutlery sets, available from most high street stores, are an economical alternative to traditional cutlery.

OPPOSITE, BOTTOM Accessorize your sink with cheap-'n'-cheerful utensils; don't hide them behind cupboard doors. Put them in easy-to-reach locations, just like these plastic fantastics, which have been hung from hooks in an apparently casual way.

When looking for functional objects at bargain prices, think about which culture has a penchant for a particular pastime – the Far East's passion for tea-drinking, for example. A trip to your local Chinatown will reveal hand-painted teapots, glazed bowls and dainty cups. For delicate tea glasses, elegant silver teapots and low-priced earthenware with colourful glazes in cumin yellow, aqua blue and russet red, try Middle Eastern stores.

Funky functional objects can easily be made to double as decoration – all they need is a showcase. For example, when it comes to crockery and teapots, you don't always have to choose plates that match. Instead, pick a colour, an era (1950s), or a pattern (geometrics), then track appropriate pieces down, creating a covetable collection to display on kitchen wall-racks or shelves.

Accessories are also about pure decoration. Objects express not only your tastes but also your wit, passions and past. Sometimes they are simple mementos: a seashell from a midwinter trip to the beach. Or they may be funny – a collection of kitsch fridge

OPPOSITE, MAIN PICTURE Look out for packaging with panache. Storage has endless accessory possibilities, as this tea caddy shows. You can find containers like these in your local Chinatown.
OPPOSITE, INSET These butter-yellow teacups make the viewer do a double-take. Transformed into a bright pair of spring bulb containers, they show how a little ingenuity goes a long way when it comes to style.
ABOVE, FAR LEFT Strings of bejewelled necklaces stored on hooks in this bedroom glamorize a white tongue-and-groove wall.
ABOVE LEFT Some accessories can be grown. Many of the best frills are provided by Mother Nature.
ABOVE For elegant silver teapots and colourful teaglasses, head for your local Middle Eastern store. Apart from tea sets, you will also find cheap ceramics, such as tagines and Moorish serving dishes.

LEFT Why leave on display an unsightly household item such as a bottle of washing-up liquid when you can hide it in a French-style milk jar? Use accessories, especially storage containers, to house kitchen bits and pieces. Chipped mugs, soft-drink cans, vases, sugar bowls – anything will do.

RIGHT Disguise and decorate. A pair of red kitchen gloves hangs over a stainless-steel pail, which conceals household cleaners. The owner has used a practical solution to add visual interest. Cleaning takes on the feel of an elegant activity rather than an onerous chore.

FAR RIGHT Instead of spending a lot of money on a regular supply of fresh flowers, accessorize your vases with permanent decorations. Dried grasses and flowers, wands and windmills, bring a twist of long-lasting colour.

INSET Use open shelving to display much loved pieces such as these covetable mugs collected on a trip to New York.

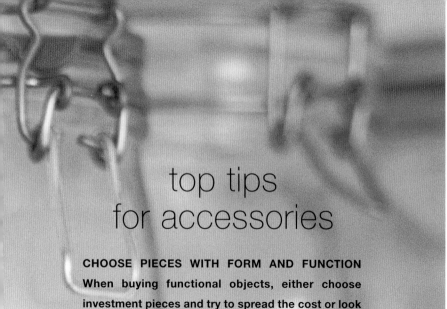

top tips for accessories

CHOOSE PIECES WITH FORM AND FUNCTION When buying functional objects, either choose investment pieces and try to spread the cost or look for good second-hand objects and stylish plastic replicas.

ABANDON THE URGE TO MATCH Instead of buying six brand-new champagne glasses, think *Breakfast at Tiffany's* and trawl second-hand shops for individual bowl-shaped glasses.

PUT FUNCTIONAL OBJECTS ON DISPLAY Hang kitchen utensils from butcher's hooks; showcase pretty teacups; leave jars of dried fruit on benches.

ACCESSORIZE, DON'T CLUTTER Place objects where they create visual surprises. One beautiful item on a shelf says more than a whole army of pieces.

ADORN YOUR HOME WITH FLOWERS Bring colour, scent and vitality indoors with bunches, sprigs and sprays of unusual and everyday flowers.

MAKE YOUR HOME A PERSONAL DIARY Decorate with things that you have collected over the years: old postcards, an alabaster cat from a holiday in Egypt, old family portraits.

ABOVE **Examples of old technologies, such as this 1930s Bakelite telephone, are one way to instil a sense of individuality and character in your home.**
LEFT **Old fruit-stewing jars have become kitchen storage containers. Seeds, pulses, nuts, pastas and other foods make eye-catching decoration, particularly when housed in sculptural transparent containers. A kitchen without food on display looks famished, so use food as an accessory.**

magnets from around the globe. And, sometimes pieces come with their own personal history – heirloom vases, for example. All sorts of things with great intrinsic worth cost next to nothing.

Items such as sculptural vases, former perfume bottles and French milk jugs can be real showstoppers. All they need is a pedestal or a shelf canvas. As interiors author Julie Iovine recommends, 'The secret of good display is to go to the extreme. Miscellaneous objects placed on a table or shelves tend to disappear. Try grouping together objects that are all of one colour or material or set one piece with an interesting shape in splendid isolation.'

Lastly, don't forget nature, which comes free in the form of driftwood, pebbles, dried grasses, and so on. Hand-picked, these can revitalize a space in an instant. Instead of conventional displays, go for big seed pods, single-stem exotic flowers or one huge vase of tulips. Plants take a small investment. Buy them young and nurture – all it takes is water, light and a bit of love.

THIS PICTURE Cushions are indispensable in any chic living space. On a practical level, they provide comfort, but as an accessory they inject colour and personality. And you can change them on a whim. Instead of buying a new shirt this season, try on a cushion instead.

LEFT A pair of unsightly bathroom radiators, which occupy a lot of wall space, have become canvases for unusual wall-hangings: a pair of tea towels decorated with plumbing motifs.

BELOW LEFT An interior's personal signature is found in the details. Some, including the wide-framed picture of a child's footprint, are purely for decoration.

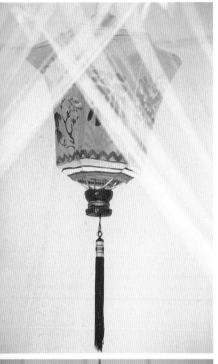

lighting

When it comes to adding chic, lighting does so much for so little, and offers many different options. Within the three categories of home illumination – general lighting, task lighting and feature lighting – there are six main tools: uplighting, downlighting, wall washing, feature lighting, colour and controls.

With general lighting, you can use any or all of the six tools to add a sense of space to your home. Lights, like colour, have the power to make a room seem bigger or smaller. For example, a soft wash from a wall sconce makes walls appear wider and larger. Downlights dotted around the edges of a ceiling can also make a small room seem more spacious.

Other ways of maximizing general light are inexpensive. Employ optical illusion by marrying mirrors with light, for example. In a bathroom, a mirror with striplights on either side will bounce light around the room. Transparent glass wall dividers and pale colour schemes also maximize light and, with it, space.

Task lighting puts practicalities first. Its purpose is to ensure that you can see what you are doing – a must when it comes to kitchen worktops or bathroom mirrors. For reading lamps and desk lights, choose portable options, which you can

ABOVE **Use a metal lampshade for a utilitarian feel or buy a standard lamp and spray it in a colour to suit your room.**
ABOVE LEFT **Trawl your local Chinatown in search of candy-coloured paper shades like this one. Japanese rice-paper shades, which come in contemporary shapes, are wonderfully kind to wallets.**
LEFT **One alternative is to reclaim and recycle. An old storm lantern, given a loving lick of red paint, lights up the life of this apartment.**
OPPOSITE **Attaching a clamp-on light to a wire provides spot illumination in this child's bedroom. There is no need for bank-busting electrical works.**

A wide variety of illumination allows you to light up your life while keeping your bank balance in the black.

THIS PICTURE All good lighting schemes, particularly in the kitchen, need to include adequate task lighting. Here a utility lamp has been hung beside a storage rack for kitchen utensils.

ABOVE RIGHT Normally an anglepoise lamp such as this French antique would be office-bound, but in this Dutch apartment it creates great task lighting for a chef.

MIDDLE RIGHT Wall sconces offer space-saving ways to create washes of light over walls. This plastic version adds form to a naked wall.

RIGHT A basic outdoor wall light has been mounted on a ceiling.

THIS PICTURE **Fairy lights give a soft, playful feel to this hard-edged interior. Strings of this type are perfect for creating coils of light in corners or garlands of light in stairwells or along hallways. Here, skeleton leaves bought from a florist are wrapped around the base of each tiny light.**

INSET **Make your own shade. Here a simple bulb has been given a makeover with a sculptural wire frame. You can go a step further and create your own light concoction with a cover of vintage fabrics or playful papers.**

LEFT A second-hand chandelier with delicately sculpted bulbs adds glitz and glamour to this living room. Find cheap reproductions or source from junk shops.
BELOW LEFT AND FAR LEFT Strands of driftwood make an elegant pendant lightshade and an eye-catching Chinese lightshade injects a twist of the exotic.

move from room to room as needed. Hallways, stairways and passageways need to be well lit. A cheap solution is to run a string of fairy lights the length of the corridor or use lengths of 'rope' lights – a run of small 'pea' bulbs set into a flexible rubber covering. These snake-like illuminations have a lamp life of 10,000 hours – approximately five years of normal use.

Feature lighting is precisely directed lighting that is used to draw the eye to a beautiful piece. Lighting can be a feature in itself, of course. A single distinctive floorlight, such as a second-hand Castiglioni 'Swan' lamp, adds grace and glamour. A second-hand chandelier, lit with candles, is also alluring.

A little inventiveness goes a long way: for funky shades, wrap 1950s fabrics around old lampshades or dot rows of different colour lightbulbs down hallways. Or think dual purpose: Tom Dixon's 'Jack' light doubles as a stool, for example. Choosing the right lightbulb for your needs also makes an enormous difference to a light's effectiveness.

Lastly, begin with the end in mind. Whether you are choosing general, task or feature lighting, plan your lighting scheme thoroughly from the outset. Putting right mistakes caused by bad planning is often the most costly exercise of all.

top tips for lighting

ENJOY NATURAL LIGHT Make the most of sunlight, moonlight and firelight. All cast a beautiful glow and bring softness and warmth into a room.

INSTALL DIMMER SWITCHES Nothing changes a room as quickly as brightening or dimming the light source. Create intimate moods in an instant.

BE INNOVATIVE String up a row of Chinese lanterns; use Christmas fairy lights at all times of the year; dot candles in antique storm lanterns around a room; invent your own shades.

LIGHT UP YOUR LIFE WITH THE RIGHT BULB Halogen bulbs are flattering for faces and provide directional light, while incandescent bulbs cast a reddish glow and are the choice for everyday use.

ECONOMIZE ON BULBS Compact fluorescent lamps (CFLs or striplights) use one quarter of the electricity used by a standard incandescent lightbulb and last up to 13 times longer.

materials

Hard materials such as wood and stone come in all shapes, sizes and prices. Before deciding how much to spend, consider these questions. How long you are likely to stay in your home? Are you renovating a property for resale? Or are you improving a rented property?

Start by writing down your needs and then plan how to get the most from your budget. Think about where you would like to spend money, but don't forget areas that need special investment. For example, whether you are staying or selling, areas of heavy wear-and-tear such as entranceways – which give visitors or prospective buyers their first impressions – need to look good. It is worth stretching your budget for floor coverings that have both beauty and longevity, such as wood, stone and high-quality woollen carpets.

When it comes to traditional materials, there are ways to achieve handsome looks for less. If you're lucky, you may find an original wooden floor hiding under a carpet, or a trip to an architectural salvage yard may yield second-hand wooden floors at bargain prices. Alternatives include less expensive softwoods such as pine, even cheaper chipboards and hardboards such as MDF, or veneers. Veneers have wood's good looks at a fraction of the price of the real thing, but a veneer floor may need to be changed once every five years.

ABOVE **A mirror-fronted medicine cabinet has been covered with colourful fridge magnets.**
ABOVE RIGHT **This cast-iron radiator has a robust look and feel. Think about the image that materials convey when choosing furniture and fittings.**
BELOW RIGHT **Many older homes have interesting features such as this rustic door. Live in a home for a while before starting to redesign and redecorate, so you can decide what you really want to keep and what you want to lose. Peel back fusty carpets and scrape off old wallpapers to see what materials lie beneath.**
OPPOSITE **Sleek stainless-steel office drawers add hi-tech utility chic to an Amsterdam apartment.**

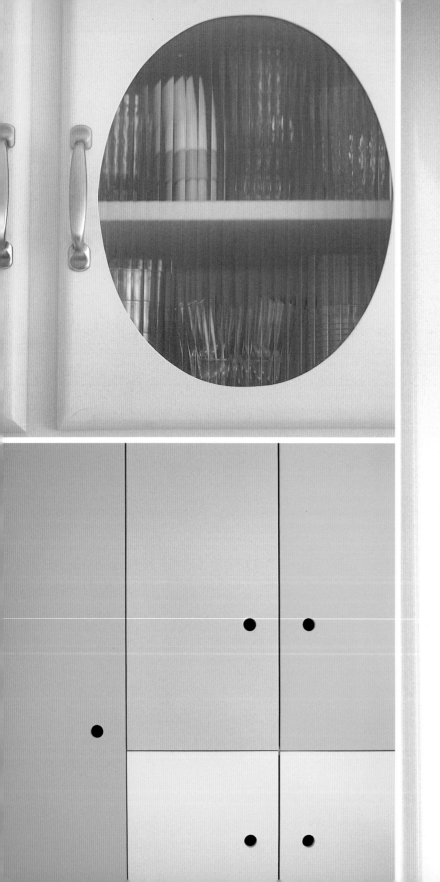

Make the most of materials at little cost by combining and contrasting. Mix rough with smooth, dark with light, and old with new.

THIS PICTURE AND INSET
Sliding corrugated plastic doors and glass bricks allow light to filter through, keeping a sense of airiness and light. Don't ignore industrial-style building materials such as these, which make inexpensive alternatives to domestic building materials. Buy from any good builders' merchant.
OPPOSITE, ABOVE LEFT **An oval corrugated-glass panel makes an eye-catching cupboard door. Textured glass allows the viewer to recognize shapes and forms without being able to discern detail.**
OPPOSITE, BELOW LEFT **Create your own kitchen cupboards from medium-density or high-density fibreboard (MDF or HDF). There are all sorts of ways to customize cupboard doors. In this kitchen, the doors are painted in various shades of blue and contrasted with cut-out holes in place of handles.**

Stone floor coverings – granite, limestone, sandstone and marble – are generally expensive. Unless you buy these materials from architectural salvage yards or discover flagstones lurking beneath an overlaid floor, it is, economically speaking, better to buy imitations. Concrete or machine-made coloured tiles, for example, cost less, are almost equally durable and come in neutral colours. Lower down the price ladder, linos and vinyls are now available in stone-like patterns. While some of these covers won't last as long as the real thing, they make attractive lookalikes.

In the early 17th century, glass was the preserve of the wealthy. While it is still a relatively expensive material, it is the most effective way of bringing more light and space into your home. There are alternatives, however. If you want glass with effects – such as etched or sand-blasted glass – you don't need to spend a fortune. For example, you can use rice paper or muslin covers to create the same feel as sand-blasted glass. Glass's cheaper cousin is plastic, which

THIS PICTURE A wall of uneven hand-made white tiles from Portugal introduces a beautiful human touch to this apartment in Amsterdam.

INSET Use materials to create a style. Sleek and shiny light woods, such as those used to construct this kitchen bench and shelf, project an image that is clean and modernist – while rough, weather-worn hardwoods add a rustic feel to an interior.

OPPOSITE, ABOVE LEFT Fake it. Instead of spending the earth on expensive materials, find convincing lookalikes such as this veneered wooden kitchen cabinet with transparent sliding doors.

OPPOSITE, BELOW, LEFT TO RIGHT A laminated worktop looks chic but costs much less than the alternatives; steel handles give a streamlined look to simple white kitchen cabinets; this galvanized-steel bucket illustrates how materials can become features in their own right.

top tips for materials

PLAN YOUR BUDGET For high-traffic areas such as hallways, spend money on good materials. If you buy too cheaply, you are likely to have to buy twice.

CUT CORNERS AND COSTS Consider alternatives to wood, stone, metal, glass, tiles and plaster. Synthetic clones such as vinyl, plastics and veneers often have similar looks at half the price.

BE OPEN-MINDED If you know the colour and feel you want, try a cheap option. Substitute chocolate-brown cork tiles for parquet floors, and opaque plastic curtains for glass screens, for example.

GO FOR NEARLY NEW Make the most of your home's existing architectural details or scour architectural salvage yards, junk yards and skips.

INVEST FOR THE FUTURE If you are planning to sell your property in the near future, invest most in the materials in the kitchen and bathroom, the two rooms that most influence house-buyers.

does the work much more cheaply in many places, such as bathroom screens and room dividers.

Metals such as stainless steel, copper and wrought iron are also reasonably expensive, but they make good investments. Although stainless-steel surfaces in the kitchen require an initial outlay, these look good year after year. Other ways to employ metals are to reuse and recycle. Harness metal's different looks – shiny, rusty, sleek or raw – and use them to advantage. Old wrought-iron bedsteads from scrapyards and antique shops make romantic headboards and footboards for basic beds, while scaffolding poles can be turned into industrial-style curtain rails.

Last but certainly not least among materials are ceramics, which encompass an array of products. Second-hand ceramics can introduce colour and pattern to your home at little cost. Whether you are using floor tiles, old Belfast sinks or broken mosaic wall coverings, ceramics are incredibly versatile and durable. In bathrooms, tiled floors and walls create cheap, hard-wearing surfaces, and white ceramic sanitaryware is smooth to the touch, sculptural – and affordable; in kitchens, tiles make hygienic easy-to-clean splashbacks.

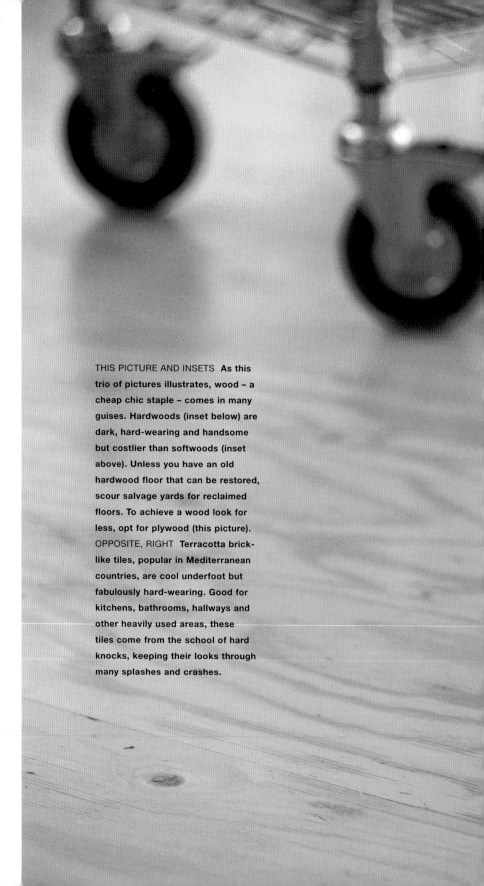

flooring

Don't let flooring absorb your entire budget. Even if you have more panache than cash, there is a good selection of low-cost floors that look and feel fabulous underfoot. Woods – both hardwoods and softwoods – are regular chart-toppers.

Hardwoods such as mahogany, teak, oak, ash and maple are generally darker and more expensive than softwoods. Architectural salvage yards and building sites are the best places to find them at affordable prices. Softwoods such as pine and cedar come in lighter shades and are cheaper – but even better value (and just as chic) are plywood and chipboard floors, made from various kinds of softwood bound with resin. For a wood feel for even less, choose veneers from DIY stores and home shops.

Wood feels warm underfoot, but does not provide the same quality of comfort as carpets and rugs. Research has shown the wisdom of investing in a carpet with a wool content of at least 80 per cent. These 80/20 wool-and-manmade-fibre mixes strike a balance between comfort, colour retention and wear. For extra comfort or to minimize wear-and-tear in high-traffic areas, rugs provide a quick, cheap solution. Alternatives to more expensive conventional woollen or Persian-style rugs are Indian cotton dhurries, tatami mats, fleece rugs and skins.

THIS PICTURE AND INSETS **As this trio of pictures illustrates, wood – a cheap chic staple – comes in many guises. Hardwoods (inset below) are dark, hard-wearing and handsome but costlier than softwoods (inset above). Unless you have an old hardwood floor that can be restored, scour salvage yards for reclaimed floors. To achieve a wood look for less, opt for plywood (this picture).** OPPOSITE, RIGHT **Terracotta brick-like tiles, popular in Mediterranean countries, are cool underfoot but fabulously hard-wearing. Good for kitchens, bathrooms, hallways and other heavily used areas, these tiles come from the school of hard knocks, keeping their looks through many splashes and crashes.**

THIS PICTURE Hexagonal white ceramic tiles make an elegant, waterproof bathroom surface. Cheap, effective bathroom surfaces include non-porous ceramic tiles, durable rubber tiles and swathes of linoleum. Unless the bathroom is for adults only, avoid wood (which warps) and carpet and rush matting (both of which rot). INSET, RIGHT A slate-grey sisal cover provides a durable foot-friendly surface for these stairs.

THIS PICTURE Concrete paving tiles have been used to make a solid, durable floor in a London kitchen. Varnished to resemble quarry tiles, they provide a neutral backdrop to everyday living.
INSET, RIGHT Square terracotta tiles form the foundation of a grand entrance. If you lay such tiles yourself, make sure the grouting is smooth and even – or the floor will require elbow grease to keep clean.

RIGHT Terracotta tiles with white grouting make a warm Mediterranean backdrop for a modern interior. Apart from walls, floors are the largest visual backdrops in your home. Avoid expensive mistakes by choosing floors that fit in with the overall colour scheme.

For spaces that need extra-durable flooring, there is nothing to beat poured concrete or concrete tiles.

THIS PICTURE **Glorious paint transforms this humdrum staircase into a striking feature. All you need is a wood primer, two layers of undercoat and a top coat. Choose high-gloss for an easy-care finish.**
ABOVE RIGHT **Royal-blue rubber adds a regal touch to a set of wooden stairs. Hard-wearing and non-slip, rubber is ideal for heavy-traffic areas.**
RIGHT AND FAR RIGHT **Wood and other hard floors are often noisy when walked on. Apart from soaking up sound, rugs, mats and dhurries are a cheap and chic way of introducing colour, texture and warmth. The white-painted floor in the picture on the far right has been softened by the addition of a knitted woollen rug.**

Natural-fibre flooring – think sisal, coir, jute, abaca and grass – is ideal if you are decorating your home on a shoestring. Use coverings made from natural fibres for entire floors or as mats and runners. Jute is the softest of these and looks like silk (perfect for bedrooms), but it is not as hardwearing as sisal, which is strong but supple (perfect for hallways and bathrooms).

The latest byword in chic is sheet flooring. Lino – as linoleum is affectionately known – with its bold and striking patterns, came into vogue in the 1920s, during the Bauhaus period. Made of flax and oil, lino has shed its dull fusty image and re-emerged as a desirable retro material. Vinyl, lino's PVC rival, has now become just as chic. Strike out with a stunning style, such as a vinyl floor embedded with photographic images of whatever you like.

Another unsung cheap chic hero is rubber flooring. Like lino and vinyl, rubber is waterproof and practical, but it also tends to be warmer, quieter and softer to the touch. Alternatively, cork, made from bark bonded with polyurethane resin, has the visual good looks of wood, but is inexpensive. It can also be painted.

For spaces that need extremely durable flooring, nothing beats poured concrete – ask your local builder to quote a price for laying a concrete floor. Stone is generally expensive, but you can find beautiful tiles that will give you the same looks for less. Tiles, too, are able to withstand countless foot treads and are available in a huge range of colourways.

Shop around for flooring. If you want to save money, don't jump on the first floor you see.

top tips for flooring

BUY THE RIGHT FLOOR FOR THE RIGHT SPACE Kitchen and bathroom floors must be durable, water-resistant, hygienic and easy-to-clean – invest in lino, rubber flooring, concrete, tiles or wood.

USE HEAVY-DUTY FLOORING FOR HIGH-TRAFFIC AREAS If you have a lino floor in the kitchen, for example, put down an extra cover such as a strip of tiles or a sisal mat in front of the sink.

PAINT WOODEN, HARDBOARD OR CHIPBOARD FLOORS Working outwards to the door, apply a wood primer, followed by two coats of undercoat and a top coat. Finish with three coats of varnish (or five in areas of heavy traffic).

USE WHAT YOU ALREADY HAVE If you have moved into an older home, you may find an original wooden floor right under your nose. Strip back old carpets to see what lies beneath.

GET LUXURY FOR LESS If you yearn for the dark browns of old wood, consider using cork tiles instead. If you want a shag-pile carpet, buy the next best thing: a luxuriously thick fleece rug (available from high-street stores).

the spaces

relaxing

LEFT AND FAR LEFT **A successfully organized living area has plenty of storage for the things that give you pleasure. To accommodate your pastimes, make the most of every space, as this homeowner has done, by creating shelving on walls and stacking books in an alcove that is too small for any other purpose.**
BELOW **Former apple crates nailed to a wall create a stylish, boxy set of shelves.**
OPPOSITE **A generously large beige modular sofa creates a useful division between the sitting and dining areas. At the end of the sofa, a space-saving nest of tables is ideal for everyday use, as well as providing surfaces for display.**

A daybed in a sunlit conservatory … a luxuriously large black leather sofa parked against a soft pink wall … a playroom by day, a home cinema by night. Spaces to relax now come in many shapes and forms. 'Living rooms' are multi-functional spaces where we unwind, watch television, play games, socialize, entertain, surf the internet, work – the list goes on and on.

If you want to design and decorate a living room for less, start by thinking carefully about what the room will be used for. While most living rooms are earmarked to accommodate a sofa and chairs, everyone's needs need to be taken into account. Will this room be primarily a place to sprawl and read? Will it be a playground and entertainment centre for rowdy children? Will you end up eating dinner there? Will you use it for work? Write down the answers to these questions, asking everyone who lives with you to contribute.

Location, location, location is the first thing to consider. In some cases, architectural solutions can make a big difference. Knocking down walls to create all-in-one spaces, conservatory extensions and loft conversions don't have to be prohibitively expensive as long as you can find an architect who appreciates the meaning of 'low budget'. Or a room swap may be in order – if, for example, the master bedroom is the most spacious room in the house and

has sun-catching bays and a disused fireplace. When you have decided where to site the living room, your next tasks are to take measurements and go out shopping.

For the room's canvases – its floors and walls – use colour and texture to maximize space and instil a mood. You know the rules: pale colours make walls appear further apart, while dark colours make them seem closer.

Create an easy-going backdrop to daily life by choosing a neutral paint or wallpaper or a pale-timber cladding. Alternatively, you could harness the emotional associations of colour to define the room's purpose: yellow and orange are conversation stimulants; blues and purples designate calm; red is perfect for an environment devoted to eating and entertaining.

ABOVE **The diva of this living room is an antique travel trunk, which doubles as a coffee table. Draped elegantly over the sofas, dust covers and old blankets make the perfect throws, softening the room's lines.** RIGHT **Forgo the traditional three-piece suite and reclaim distinctive pieces. A black-painted wooden fisherman's chest stands in front of a metal Detroit gilder bench, a former 1960s porch favourite, while to the right is a 1930s leather club chair.**

RIGHT AND BELOW RIGHT The hearth was traditionally the heart of the home. Even in rooms where the hearth is no longer used for a fire, the eye is always drawn towards it. Instead of concealing a disused fireplace, use the alcove to display objects of visual interest such as those illustrated here – an autumnal display of gourds and twisted branches, and a row of retro paper bags that double as magazine tidies.

THIS PICTURE **A vintage Venetian chandelier makes a glamorous centrepiece in this light, airy living room. Leaving the room free of curtains and painting its walls and floors white is a simple way to create a feeling of incredible spaciousness. Optical illusions can reduce your building bills: why knock down a wall when a coat of light-coloured paint produces the same result?**

At the end of a long day's work, there is nothing more satisfying than kicking off your shoes. The kindest underfoot solution for weary feet is a carpet or rug. Indian dhurries, second-hand Persian carpets and high-street weaves are gentle on the purse as well as the feet, but have the advantage of introducing softness, style and colour. Other low-cost solutions include rugs made from second-hand carpets with the edges turned over or bound, sheepskins or soft natural fibres such as jute.

The next big element to consider is furnishings. If you plan to do a lot of entertaining, you need furniture that is flexible and easy to move, perhaps arranged around a central focus such as a fireplace or a coffee table. If the living room doubles as a work room, you may want to think about installing a fold-away table that can be hidden in a cupboard in the evenings when no longer needed.

Create an easy-going backdrop with a neutral paint or wallpaper or a pale-timber cladding.

ABOVE RIGHT **A Biedermeier bateau-style sofa provides seating for several, while a wooden garden chair is easily opened up to create another place to rest. For cheap chic seating, reclaim outdoor furniture and bring it indoors. White household candles in candelabra add style. The floor light is homemade from a clamp-on lamp attached to a stand.**
RIGHT AND FAR RIGHT **You can use a stove to heat a room, as this homeowner has. The former fireplace has contemporary good looks, right down to its smooth modern mantelpiece lined with *objets d'art*.**

High-street retail outlets have a good selection of adaptable armchairs and sofas – particularly if you want a fold-out spare bed – at reasonable prices. To give mass-produced pieces of furniture a more individual character, simply sew your own covers out of vintage fabrics or dress them with throws bought from second-hand shops; or use old scarves, tartan blankets, an assortment of colourful cushions, cast-off bedspreads or ethnic fabrics such as Indonesian batik fabrics or Indian saris. Rescue and revive antique leather sofas,

ABOVE **Neutral colours such as grey, taupe and beige contrast with vibrant dandelion yellows, fresh greens and highlights of red to create an inspirational living space. Fabrics, including the soft sheepskins and coloured rugs, add texture. The sliding door, painted in bold blocks of colour, is made from reclaimed wood.**

THIS PICTURE For family living areas, use movable furniture to accommodate everyone's needs. If you move house, you can always take it with you. A television on castors is easily tucked away, while the red pouf is extra seating or a foot rest.
RIGHT AND INSET Create visual interest at next to no expense. Instead of papering your entire room, cover a single wall with a vintage paper, as the owner has done in this Amsterdam home. Here a large pine storage chest doubles as a daybed. For cheap chic art, ask a budding Leonardo to draw you a picture.

OPPOSITE This tucked-away living area in a garden cottage makes the most of the space available. From the chinoiserie lampshade to the pale blue coffee table, the look is light, fresh and contemporary. The vertical lines of the white tongue-and-groove walls and the horizontal lines on the ceiling make the room appear larger than it is.

RIGHT Dress your couch in a little reversible number. Striped canvas meets exotic floral in this example of a cushion cover sewn from recycled fabrics.

FAR RIGHT Instead of buying cut flowers, grow plants from bulbs or seeds and just add water.

BELOW Garden-plucked red roses displayed in a former vinegar bottle cost nothing but add much.

BELOW RIGHT Make your own sofa. Transform an old second-hand bed into a laid-back sofa with a colourful canvas cover. Adorn it with an entourage of pillows and cushions in different shapes and sizes.

ABOVE **An eclectic combination of covers – from zebra stripes and blue velvet to broderie anglaise and chinoiserie – make the ingredients of a cushion party on this stylish sofa. Among the wall decorations is a stencil of a moose head beside favourite photographs.**
RIGHT **A hot-pink artificial flower head broken up into petals and threaded onto a piece of blue string creates a low-cost, high-impact garland.**
OPPOSITE, ABOVE **A plain white sofa cover dyed a bright aqua blue is the focal point of this light and airy sitting room. Old intact sofa covers have no sell-by date – all they need, as here, is a darker dye.**
OPPOSITE, BELOW **A sheer voile curtain diffuses the light in this living room, giving the whole space an ethereal quality. With such a translucent backdrop, the floor, coated in a thick glossy paint, also reflects the light. A grand display of flowers on the table adds colour, glamour, scent and chic.**

which last a lifetime, from junk shops, car-boot sales and salvage yards. Other options for stylish seating including chaises longues, slouchy armchairs, garden seats, wicker chairs, church pews and antique leather club chairs. For contemporary retro looks, chic alternatives include colourful beanbags, low-slung plastic seats, and inflatable blow-up sofas and armchairs softened with 1960s-style cushions.

For low-cost, contemporary-looking storage, choose an inexpensive modular system of the type that can be found in most large furniture warehouses. Flat-packed shelves and units are also kind on your budget and can easily be given a facelift with a coat of paint. Among other resurrected storage options are old wardrobes, 1960s sideboards, simple ottomans, chests and trunks. For smaller storage for videos and CDs, try former hat boxes, shoeboxes and wine boxes.

Don't forget that relaxing areas are often public spaces where you are likely to entertain visitors. They are ideal settings in which to showcase the things you love and objects that have special meaning for you – such items may provide conversational starting points. Fresh flowers always make a room welcoming.

Efficient lighting costs little but adds much. During the day, maximize natural daylight by extending windows and adding skylights. During the evening, use a combination of lighting solutions such as floor lamps, wall lights and reading lights. Create a sense of theatre. The living room is, after all, a backdrop for life.

top tips for relaxing

FASHION A STYLE Reinvent a look or create your own style and accessorize. For example, think faded grandeur (peeling paint effects, gilt frames), modern natural (leather sofas, muslin curtains) or new retro (inflatable sofas, plastic chairs, vintage geometric cushions).

BE INVENTIVE WITH LIGHTING If your living room has a pendant light, put it on a dimmer switch, replace it with a gothic-style candelabrum lit by candles or install an unlit feature such as a glittery second-hand chandelier.

USE FABRICS FOR COMFORT Add a splash of colour with curtains sewn from old scarves, make cushions from old sweaters, re-upholster sofa covers or dress the floor with a Mexican rug.

MAKE MONEY If you have cash to invest, buy 20th-century collectables. An Eames lounger bought five years ago has almost trebled in value since. Trawl second-hand stores for pieces by designers such as Robin Day, Verner Panton, Arne Jacobsen and Philippe Starck.

REVAMP THE HEARTH If you have an empty fireplace, restore it with a second-hand insert and surround. For the same effect without the cost, put a mixture of large church candles and small tealights in the fireplace.

cooking and eating

Cooking and eating: two essential, pleasurable activities that can be accommodated both cheaply and chicly. Traditionally, in better off households, these spaces were almost always separated – but, as informality has replaced protocol, stiff-upper-lipped dining rooms have generally come to be regarded as dinosaurs. Modern life has married cooking and eating spaces into one – ideally, large – room.

What kind of arrangement you choose for preparing and eating meals in your home depends on your lifestyle and the people you live with. If you eat out a lot, a well-organized galley kitchen with breakfast bar, stools, a compact refrigerator and microwave may be enough to satisfy your needs. For people who share their home with family or friends, an area that can accommodate both cooking and dining is the perfect place to catch up at the beginning and end of the day. To create such an area, you may need to knock down a wall between the kitchen and a living room, dining room or hallway. Architectural changes can be expensive, but, in this case, introducing extra light and space and creating fluidity between rooms is worth its weight in gourmet meals.

ABOVE AND OPPOSITE **A wall of white Portuguese tiles visually marks out the kitchen area in this one-room living space. The freestanding unit swallowed most of the budget, but it will last for years.**
ABOVE CENTRE **Old bottles with coloured glass or curvaceous shapes make good vases.**
ABOVE LEFT **Post office sorting shelves have been given a new purpose in life as kitchen storage. Open shelving of this type costs a lot less than a fitted kitchen.**
BELOW **A dark veneer has been added to the doors of this kitchen to give it a 1970s look in keeping with the rest of the building.**

Minimalist, retro chic and farmhouse looks are the best value.

ABOVE **The centrepiece of this table is a wine cooler that has been transformed into a stylish vase. The owner made his own table out of plywood. He also built the floor-to-ceiling cupboard, which provides oodles of seamless storage space.**

LEFT **Bespoke plywood doors have been installed to separate a kitchen from a dining area in this small apartment.**

OPPOSITE, ABOVE **Customize second-hand kitchen appliances in a colour that suits your appetite. Use car spray or enamelled paint.**

OPPOSITE, BELOW **Minimal shelves add horizontal stripes of colour to a white wall. Open shelving of this kind gives you the opportunity to keep all your kitchen essentials on display as well as making them easily accessible.**

the spaces

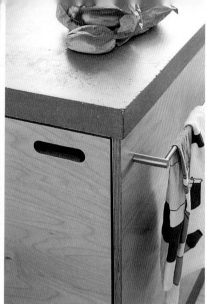

RIGHT **The frame around an extractor fan becomes a structural feature in this kitchen when an array of utensils are hung from it.**

FAR RIGHT **Holes in cupboard doors are a cheaper alternative to handles.**

OPPOSITE **Everything in this kitchen comes from the high street. The owner has imaginatively exploited all the available space, with tall cupboards reaching up to the ceiling. Chic accessories include a Dualit toaster – an investment buy that comes with a guarantee that it will outlive its owner.**

BELOW **The backdrop to this kitchen is a favourite photograph reproduced as wallpaper by a specialist printer. A glossy plywood floor creates a good-value, hard-working kitchen surface. Note how the wall storage reaches right up to the ceiling.**

Start by deciding on your kitchen layout, bearing in mind that most kitchens are based on the tried and tested L-shape or U-shape. Make a list of the appliances and fittings you would like to include and decide where you are going to put them, then work out your budget. Once you've made a room plan and done your homework, it is time to grab your largest shopping bag.

High-street shops and large home stores have low-cost, off-the-peg modern kitchen carcasses. To give them personality, simply accessorize. Or you can fashion your own kitchen from low-cost materials. For example, have cupboards built from cheap, medium-density fibreboard (MDF) to create a neat, stylish effect. A joiner or carpenter will construct a carcass for you, perhaps from MDF's more hard-working cousin, high-density fibreboard (HDF), with doors made from MDF, which you can customize with handles and paint. Use laminates for retro worktops and linoleum for flooring; lino makes an attractive kitchen feature for more splash and less cash than the alternatives.

The next subject to consider is the style of your fixtures and fittings. High-tech lovers: stop! Don't do it. Sleek, sophisticated elements of this style such as shiny stainless steel and smooth granite cost a bomb. Much better for your budget are minimalist, retro chic and rustic farmhouse looks.

A minimalist effect is dependent on efficient storage, so take this into account when planning, and remember the basics such as a rubbish bin. If you build in lots of drawers and hidden pull-outs, it's easy to make the most of every inch of space. For crockery and ceramics, choose nothing but white from high-street and chain stores.

The modern retro feel combines cheap materials such as painted wood, checked linos and pastel colours. Hunt down pastel-painted wood and Formica freestanding cabinets from the 1950s and 1960s, and retro accessories such as graphically decorated teacups and teapots. It is also worth looking out for pastel-coloured and retro refrigerators.

The farmhouse style fits in with the modern trend for dual-purpose spaces. The main requisite of this type of kitchen is its centrepiece, the table: for a rustic feel, choose an old refectory table or a large

THIS PICTURE **A fresh linen tablecloth and a second-hand candelabrum are all it takes to give this kitchen eating area a formal feel. The most striking feature of the room is the large open plate rack, a simple, easy-to-make device for showing off serving dishes and trays. Above the rack, an Indian garland made of tin frames the room.**

pine table and cover it with a flat-weave cloth. An old butler's sink complete with reclaimed taps is another essential. Instead of buying high-tech modern kitchen equipment, go for early examples of gadgets such as coffee grinders, glass juicers, nutcrackers, herb cutters and weighing scales with sets of brass or iron weights. Similarly, sets of old tea strainers, enamel colanders, rolling pins and aluminium pots and pans are satisfying to use and display.

Whatever you choose, ensure that it is classic, since fashion fads are a waste of time and money. When it comes to building, decorating and preparing your kitchen, it pays to make the most of anything that's free such as natural light and features. As the former Sugar Club chef Peter Gordon says, 'It's fantastic working in natural light – it makes preparation much easier and more fun.' So put worktops or sinks under windows or install skylights.

Lighting essentials include adequate task lighting over worktops and stoves. For all-in-one spaces, you need flexibility. Dimmer switches can be used to change mood, creating a soft glow for eating or a bright light for cooking. For dining, use candles to give a sense of ritual. Dimmer switches, drop lighting and wall lights also enhance a sense of occasion.

For walls, the solution may be just beneath that horror show of wallpaper. Expose bricks to add to a rustic look. Most kitchen walls need a wipeable waterproof surface. The cheapest option is paint, but veneer works equally well. Instead of expensive stone tiles, decorate a wall with hardwood ply; you need to seal and paint it.

ABOVE **From the yellow-upholstered chairs to the blue shelf in the background, this eating area has been designed as an enjoyable place to be. A second-hand leather sofa provides an area to sit and chat. On the table are handmade placemats cut from colourful felt, while a driftwood lampshade from South Africa crowns the table.**
ABOVE RIGHT **Paint your fridge with chalk board paint, as this owner has done, and use it to write shopping lists and messages – or simply draw your dreams.**
ABOVE FAR RIGHT **Instead of forking out on crockery, use cheap-'n'-cheerful plastic picnic plates.**
OPPOSITE **Make the most of basics such as these stripy tea towels and chinoiserie thermoses. Think laterally about kitchen furniture. A set of drawers, once earmarked for a bedroom, are equally at home here.**

ABOVE **Efficient kitchens have ample storage. Here a disused stairwell has become a kitchen cupboard containing everything but the kitchen sink.**

ABOVE RIGHT **Mix old and new. Keep what you have, but add a modern twist. In this kitchen, above the old gas cooker is a smart new extractor fan, and a sleek zinc worktop crowns a rough wooden cupboard.**

RIGHT **White crockery never goes out of style.**

OPPOSITE, ABOVE **Floor-to-ceiling cupboards provide an abundance of storage space in this minimalist kitchen. Again, holes are used instead of handles to give easy access to the contents of drawers and cupboards at next to no cost.**

OPPOSITE, BELOW **The bright and breezy palette of blond wood and white paint in this kitchen maximizes the impression of space.**

Particular areas – stove and sink splashbacks and worktops, for example – need durable, hard-working surfaces. Ceramic, hard-glazed tiles, used in combination with an epoxy grout and water-resistant resin, make low-cost, easy-to-maintain worktops. If you have a little money to invest, marble is the chef's choice.

The most important piece of furniture in any dining area is the table, the bigger the better. While inexpensive tables are available from high-street stores, you can always use glass desks or make your own from a smooth door mounted on trestles.

To enjoy long, lingering lunches to the full, your guests will need comfortable seats. For alternative shoestring seating, buy old church pews, use rustic garden furniture seats, old school chairs or fold-out picnic chairs, or reupholster retro chairs. To soften hard edges, simply fashion cushions to fit.

As for hardware – ovens, dishwashers and fridges – the cheapest option is to buy second-hand. Kitchens are often the last rooms that people selling their homes redesign and redecorate in order to attract buyers – and kitchen appliances may be the first things new owners rip out – so it is not too difficult to find second-hand hardware of reasonably good quality. Otherwise, look out for lesser known brands, which sell more cheaply – or compromise: if you eat out a lot, you can probably make do with a microwave rather than an oven.

top tips for cooking and eating

PLAN TO MAKE PERFECT Before you part with a penny, define exactly what you want from your kitchen. In the long run, you'll save yourself time, heartache and money.

MAKE A NOMADIC DINING ROOM To transform any room into an impromptu dining room, go Eastern. Mount a smooth door on bricks, cover it with a sheet or an ethnic cloth, and strew cushions around it on the floor.

USE BIG IDEAS FOR SMALL SPACES If your cooking and eating area is small, use optical illusion to enlarge it: choose reflective surfaces and glass tables; use a pale colour scheme. For extended vistas, hang a mirror above the dining area.

MAKE WORKTOPS WORK It's worth spending money on high-quality worktops, which bear the brunt of hard work and are a nuisance to replace. Investment choices include marble, granite, hardwoods and stainless steel.

PROTECT HARD-WEAR AREAS If you don't have the budget to invest in a good worktop or floor, get the next best thing. Buy take-away marble slabs and thick wooden chopping boards, and put rubber mats in front of sinks.

sleeping

Bedrooms are usually the last rooms to receive our attention when it comes to interior design. Yet sleep is one of the most important things we do. Studies have shown that, for every hour's sleep we forfeit each week, we reduce our IQ by one point. Getting a good night's sleep is vital to both our well-being and our intelligence.

Transforming a bedroom into a haven doesn't have to be ruinously expensive. Most bedrooms are simple spaces, where the bed takes centre stage. While clothes-aholics might give priority to installing a walk-in wardrobe, most of us accept that our bedroom also needs to serve as our dressing room. To create a restful but hard-working space, the trick is to blend practicalities – such as capacious clothes storage – with aesthetics.

The first thing you must invest in for health's sake is a decent bed. Most sleep experts advise buying a new bed every ten years. If the cost hurts, make it easier to endure by thinking of the money spread over the next decade. A supportive, well-cushioned bed is fundamental to a good night's sleep. Choose 'pocket sprung' mattresses (mattresses sprung with individual coils) to give your

OPPOSITE **A simple racking system creates eye-catching storage for everything from the ironing board to bedside tables. Simple ingenuity has been used to transform an everyday object into a piece of art.**
ABOVE **Puppets, a little girl's dress, and a hot water bottle line up along this picture-perfect plywood racking system.**
ABOVE, INSET **This bed consists of a good-quality mattress mounted on wooden slats, which in turn rest on a base of outdoor building blocks.**
LEFT **A generously sized bed is mounted on old railway sleepers, and the weathered-wood theme is carried through to the teak headboard and the bedside tables, made from a block of oak. Flanking the bed are two antique inspection lamps.**

111

ABOVE **Lengths of muslin draped over the bed in the style of mosquito nets add an exotic twist to this little girl's room. A paper lampshade provides a crown of colour. Bed ends like these often turn up in second-hand markets.**

spine the support it needs. And don't stop at the mattress. Make sure your pillows won't give you nightmares. Invest in the best to ensure your neck and head are adequately supported.

Where you can make savings is on your bed linen and coverings. Pure linen makes a soporific sleeping partner, but it is expensive to buy new. Save yourself wallet-ache by picking up antique or second-hand sheets from markets, or sew white linen tablecloths together. A less expensive option, cotton (particularly Egyptian cotton) is soft against naked skin, bought ready-to-wear from high-street stores.

To dress your bed, buy second-hand woollen blankets or stitch together old woollen scarves to create a patchwork cover. For decoration, make a collage of old scarves, fabric off-cuts, picnic blankets, light rugs and vintage curtains. Instead of a traditional patchwork of hundreds of tiny squares, choose four big blocks of complementary fabrics.

A duvet is an investment buy. The quality and type of feathers in a duvet affects the price, but you can console your wallet by offsetting the cost with low-priced covers, either bought from the high street or hand-made by you – all you need is two cotton sheets sewn together and dyed fast in your most-loved colour.

To create a tranquil environment, ambience is everything. Keep lighting soft, intimate and romantic. All you really need is a bedside light. Just buy an old lamp and revamp it with foxy fabrics or pick a retro classic from a second-hand shop. Most bedrooms have a central pendant light. Dress it for less with a glamorous second-hand chandelier or a Chinese paper lampshade. For instant changes of mood, install a dimmer switch.

ABOVE **Bedrooms often need to double as dressing rooms. Instead of hiding all your gorgeous pieces, put them out on show, making a feature of, for example, a row of shoes.**
LEFT **Fairy lights frame built-in open shelves, which house everything that a little girl needs to keep close at hand.**

THIS PICTURE Bedrooms need to be soporific spaces. Nothing is kinder to budgets than a pared-back minimalist look, as represented by this attic bedroom painted in peaceful white. Apart from the bed, second-hand and vintage books are its only feature, perfectly placed for bedside reading.

INSET Bedrooms are fabric magnets. Instead of standard bedding, seek alternatives to sleep with, such as vintage shawls, tartan blankets, antique linens, tablecloths and saris.

THIS PICTURE Although it looks a million dollars, this bedroom was not expensive to put together. Plenty of large, soft pillows, pristine white cottons, and a huge body-length mirror add decadent notes. A minimal white shelf makes a stylish floating side table. Instead of fitting a new carpet, the owners have used a big square of carpet with bound edges. When they leave, it can roll up and roll out the door.

RIGHT Linen tablecloths bought at a sale make a stylish cover for this bed.
BELOW The curtains are made from army tent fabric, which keeps in the warmth but blocks out the light. A shell garland is draped around a wall-mounted bedside light.
BELOW CENTRE A fabric print has been cut out and nailed to a canvas. To make a similar one, seek out funky bolts of graphic fabric.
BELOW RIGHT A bedside table can be as simple as this second-hand rustic stool. An old office light makes a perfect reading lamp.

Bedside tables for your lights are another necessity. For a cheap, rustic-style table, sand and varnish an old tree trunk or adapt a coffee table, adding a linen handkerchief to dress it. Upturned crates covered with a paisley silk scarf also make chic side tables for a snip.

When it comes to sleep, windows need to be adequately covered. Darkness helps your body to secrete the hormone melatonin, which aids sleep. For total blackout, choose thick fabrics such as denim, canvas or velvet and sew blackout material to the side of the curtain facing the window. Shutters bought second-hand and off-the-peg blinds cut to fit also keep rooms in the dark.

The soles of your feet crave warmth and softness. Investing in a carpet is the foot-friendly thing to do, but a less expensive option is

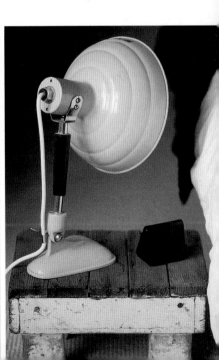

THIS PICTURE This striped wall was inspired by the colours of a babygro (see page 20). Where painting a whole room would be overpowering, painting a single wall can transform the ordinary into something extraordinary. Reclaimed wooden shelving, second-hand cupboards and a vintage dog-on-wheels are just some of the junk finds that cost next to nothing. For extra hanging space, hooks have been added to the side of the clothes cupboard. The smooth white top of the cabinet is the ideal place for a photo gallery.

THIS PICTURE It's smarter to barter. The old doors in
this bedroom were swapped for a bottle of wine. The
disused fireplace alcove, with its exposed brick,
becomes an installation display area.

INSET A simple bare wire becomes the perfect place
from which to hang children's clothes. A sheepskin on
the floor adds warmth to bare boards.

ABOVE Painting the whole fireplace white makes it look like a sculptural relief. White brings with it a sense of peace – the feel of a retreat extends to the accessories, including the chic aromatherapy burner on the mantelpiece.

ABOVE LEFT This fabric-and-wood-framed wardrobe is a cheap and ingenious way to store clothes and shoes without losing a sense of space. Save money on bedroom storage by using every nook and cranny.

LEFT Mix old and new, something plain and something blue. A combination of florals looks soft and pretty.

OPPOSITE An all-white and neutral colour scheme pushes the walls outwards in this serene bedroom. Even the quietly patterned bed linen and pale-coloured blanket contribute to the restful palette. To enhance the impression of space, all accessories are strictly white, including the wall-mounted light.

The bedroom is the most important place in the home, but often receives the least attention.

to buy a rug to put by the bed. Sheepskin, wool or silk rugs are the kindest to sleepy feet. For general wallet-friendly flooring, try wood veneers or natural fibre carpeting such as jute. You'll just need a pair of slippers nearby.

To sleep soundly, perchance to dream, it helps to decorate your bedroom in quiet, calming colours. For colour on a budget, you'll need a pot of paint or strips of wallpaper in peaceful patterns and textures. Florals from the 1950s, paisleys and chinoiserie papers are currently back in vogue: buy vintage papers or reproductions from the high street.

For mental peace you need your bedroom to be tidy and well ordered, which means good storage. Make the most of disused spaces, such as the space under the bed, or create a roomy wardrobe by bringing in the walls with floor-to-ceiling storage, made seamless with push-catch doors.

Clothes need their own home. Again, there's no need to spend a fortune on furniture. A simple open clothes rack and stylish boxes can be used to make low-cost storage. Keep shoes in the boxes they came in, but for display decorate the boxes with retro wallpapers. And don't forget alternative clothes storage such as former office filing cabinets for drawers, stacked tea chests, medicine cabinets and book shelves.

With such a chic bedroom – put together on a shoestring – you will be able to hit the pillow at night without taking a hit on your bank account.

ABOVE **This freestanding wardrobe also serves as a bedhead. Behind it, open shelves provide storage for pairs of shoes. Rather than hide your beautiful dresses behind closed doors, bring them out to create decorative features. Change the display as often as you change your clothes.**
RIGHT **Instead of a bedside light, use a garland of fairylights woven around metal bed ends.**
OPPOSITE, ABOVE **You don't need a bathroom attached to your master bedroom when you can have a rolltop French-style bateau bath in your boudoir.**
OPPOSITE, BELOW **A bright Asian kite has landed on this bedroom wall, introducing a splash of colour. As an alternative to buying bookcases, simply stack books or magazines on top of each other. Adorn walls with anything that catches the eye, from postcards to beads, as illustrated here.**

top tips for sleeping

INVEST IN REST Spend most of your budget on the best bed money can buy. Before buying, lie down on the bed in the showroom for 15 minutes or more, testing different positions for comfort.

ACCESSORIZE FOR LESS Buy good-quality sheets from antique linen shops or brand-new cotton sheets from high-street stores. Adorn your bed with beautiful homemade covers.

RECYCLE, REUSE AND REINVENT Customize an office filing cabinet and turn it into drawers; store bed linen in an old tea chest; hang a painted broomstick on two long lengths of sturdy string from ceiling hooks and use it as a clothes rack.

GO ZEN One of the most stylish (and cheapest) looks for bedrooms is pure Zen. Clear all surfaces, paint walls in a pale colour and choose white and neutral accessories. If possible, stash clothes in a floor-to-ceiling cupboard.

DRESS SENSE Hang out your glad rags on a rack and colour-coordinate, or turn your collection of handbags into art and hang them off wooden clothes pegs spaced evenly along a wall.

bathing

Since its emergence from behind locked doors, the bathroom has received a fundamental makeover. No longer regarded as simply a functional place for washing at the beginning and end of the day, it has become somewhere to relax and luxuriate. But, while designers such as Philippe Starck and Jasper Morrison have given the once-shy bathroom a revamp, the good news is that you don't have to pay designer-label prices to have a chic, sleek home retreat.

When planning a bathroom, go back to basics. Where is the best place in your home for a bathroom? Could you convert a spare bedroom or loft space? Or does your existing small bathroom have everything, albeit at a squeeze? If the master bedroom is vast, is it possible to sacrifice a corner to create an ensuite shower? Modern off-the-peg shower cubicles can be installed virtually anywhere with the right plumbing – under a staircase or in a hall cupboard, for example. Save yourself time and money by being clear in your own mind about your priorities.

Next, give a thought to practicalities such as electrical outlets, drainpipes, plumbing regulations and ventilation systems – all of which must comply with local regulations. It is crucial to get these details right now, since alterations at a later stage are likely to be costly and disruptive. Regulations vary from area to area, so seek advice from a local professional.

Practical considerations aside, it is time to start thinking about how to make your bathroom design 'budget friendly'. Start with the biggest spaces – the floors and walls. Think about who will use the bathroom. For example, young children love to splash water

ABOVE **A picture holdall has taken on a new life as a laundry bag. The sleek, hygienic feel of this bathroom is complemented by a utilitarian metal lampshade from the high street.**
TOP **For cheap chic, nothing beats standard sanitaryware such as this handbasin, which is easy to accessorize.**
ABOVE RIGHT **Matching tiles on bathtub and walls create a seamless, hotel-like look.**

OPPOSITE **This fibreglass bath is lighter than the traditional cast-iron variety and keeps water warm for longer, reducing hot-water bills. If you want your bath to double as a shower, save money by buying a plastic shower curtain rather than a glass screen. Concrete plant pots beside the bath make a home for accessories.**
BELOW **Bathroom storage needn't be boring – as this former printer's shelf lined with lotions and potions illustrates.**

RIGHT **An awkward alcove has been put to clever use in this business-like bathroom. As well as providing extra storage space, it has been transformed into a display cabinet for bathroom essentials such as rolled-up towels, lotions and potions, and for decorative items such as framed pictures. The cane basket tucked away on the bottom shelf is used to conceal less attractive bathroom items. Underneath the handbasin is a towel rack, which again makes imaginative use of otherwise useless space.**

OPPOSITE, BELOW **Built-in storage is invaluable in a bathroom. One way to create it is by installing drawers and cupboards in the space underneath a handbasin or around a lavatory cistern.**

everywhere, so in a bathroom used by children avoid carpet (which rots) and softwoods (which warp). Better alternatives are rubber tiles, lino and non-glazed, non-slip ceramic tiles, which are hygienic, durable and water-resistant. For an adults-only bathroom, the choice widens to include varnished softwoods, wood veneers and rubber-backed, bathroom-quality carpets made from cotton or synthetic fibres.

Wall coverings must be damp-proof and hygienic, but they can also be used to influence a room's architecture. For example, if your bathroom is an odd shape, you can make it look more regular with a monochrome paint scheme. While white is a common bathroom choice, it can look reminiscent of a doctor's surgery. Use pastels to introduce colour without reducing the sense of space. Waterproof paints are the cheapest wall coverings, but machine-made tiles and tongue-and-groove panelling are effective, inexpensive alternatives. Again, play architect with visual effects. A long, thin room looks wider with big square tiles.

ABOVE **A Zen-like feel – where everything is light, clean and pared back to a minimum –** enhances the serenity of this room. A tall medicine cabinet offers an elegant solution to hiding clutter, while a huge mirror above the bath adds a whole new dimension of space.

LEFT **Terracotta brick flooring – which can be had for a song from local builders' merchants – sets up an interesting visual and textural contrast to glossy white tiles in this utilitarian bathroom, which makes excellent use of natural light. Instead of a dressing mirror, the owner has installed the only item of this type that he really needs: a simple shaving mirror.**

Acquiring a top-quality bathtub doesn't have to cost more than a Christmas shopping expedition. The most important thing is to find a bath that's comfortable – so, if you are thinking of buying new, try out various models in the showroom before parting with your money. Traditional white ceramic bath suites are relatively inexpensive. What's more, you can find them in all sorts of shapes and sizes. Entire suites are now designed for tiny bathrooms, with corner and sit tubs becoming very popular. The set doesn't have to match. In fact, investing in one covetable piece, such as a wall-mounted glass or conical wooden basin, can give a bathroom an impressive centrepiece.

Instead of buying a set of shiny new matching pieces, you may want to add interest with reclaimed bathroom fittings. Scour salvage yards for all sorts of treasures, such as reclaimed bathtubs. If you particularly desire a roll-top, bateau-style bath, ensure that the enamel is in good condition or it many prove expensive to repair. Keep your eyes open for Belfast sinks, huge daisy-head shower

RIGHT, TOP TO BOTTOM **To make toothbrush holders, simply drill holes in blocks of wood. Natural accessories such as this wooden light-pull add individual character to a bathroom. A pebble found on the beach serves as a shower-door handle.**
OPPOSITE **Plywood panelling has been installed to give these bathroom walls the visual warmth of wood. As a modern counterpoint to the reclaimed handbasin frame, the owners have accessorized with a Philippe Starck tap and basin for a sleek contemporary look. In the corner, an old enamel bucket makes a good container for other bathroom sundries.**

THIS PICTURE AND INSET **In this funky bathroom, acrylic paint stencils add colour and pattern to the wall and the panelled side of the bath. A weathered wood block nailed to a wall has become an off-beat toilet-roll holder, while wire-netting shelves offer an easily accessible, see-through storage solution.**

OPPOSITE **A enlarged photo of blossom has been made into a wall hanging, enhancing the sense of space in this room. Pictures of landscapes and natural objects are a clever low-cost way to create blue-sky horizons in a small room. An old roll-top bath has been given a new lease of life with a coat of matt-black paint.**

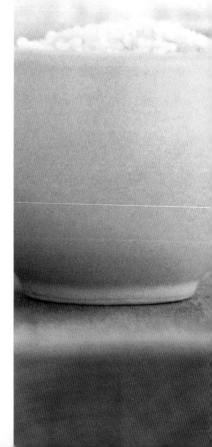

attachments and Victorian lavatories. Among other sources of inspiration are former hospital pieces – taps, spouts and cabinets, for example – which perfectly complement a bathroom's sanitary appearance and feel.

A cheap way to keep your bathroom looking chic is to banish all clutter, keeping only a few beautiful items on view. For a pared-down Zen look, build a cupboard flush with a wall – this can also be used to disguise an ugly cistern. All you need is wood cut to size at your local DIY shop and fitted with push-click closures, so that, when installed, the cupboard looks like a flat wall.

Another trick is to disguise storage by hiding shelves behind a big brash shiny mirror, or have your handbasin built into the top of a long, square cupboard.

For accessories, the most economical approach, as so often, is to reclaim, reuse and recycle. An old butterdish makes a great soap tray; use a pretty vase as a toothbrush holder; employ a rustic railway sleeper as a shelf for lotions and potions. Decoration can cost no more than a walk on the beach. Collect objects such as striped pebbles, speckled seashells and sculptural driftwood and put them on display.

ABOVE AND ABOVE LEFT **Beige mosaic tiles have been used to make stylish waterproof walls. A durable rubber floor like this one is relatively easy to lay and provides an excellent splashproof surface. In the corner, a woven net bag – a cheap purchase from a street market – has been put to good use as a child's toy tidy.**
OPPOSITE, ABOVE **Compact fittings specially made for small bathrooms make efficient use of precious centimetres in this pint-sized room.**
OPPOSITE, BELOW **Open shelving set into the cupboard doors means that towels and vases are accessible while other less lovely toiletries are stashed out of sight. Shelving installed elsewhere in the room has been cut down from a kitchen work surface.**

top tips for bathing

LET THERE BE LIGHT Make as much use as you can of natural light. Install skylights or extend windows, covering them with opaque blinds.

MAXIMIZE SPACE WITH OPTICAL ARTISTRY Hang a big, light-deflecting mirror near a light; bounce light off shiny surfaces; or dot recessed ceiling lights around the perimeter of the ceiling.

BRIGHTEN UP A quick and simple way to add colour and texture to a dull bathroom is to buy colourful towels, bath mats and shower curtains.

GO DUAL-PURPOSE Stylish radiators make great towel rails, for example – or you could build a storage chest from MDF with a hinged lid that doubles as a seat.

SAVE MONEY, ADD STYLE Scour junk shops for classic bathroom accessories. Swap modern taps for reconditioned originals; find old tile-backed washstands; discover vintage toothbrush holders, soap dishes and towel rails.

working

With the personal computer almost as common as the kitchen sink, the 'home office' has become for many of us the place where we not only work but also shop, bank, make travel arrangements and email friends. For others, the home office is simply a quiet place to write letters and pay bills.

There is no getting away from the fact that home computers and associated technology are expensive, but you can save money on the office itself. If you are starved of space, the kitchen table can become a home office by day and a food preparation area by night. A capacious bed makes working from between the sheets another option – with breakfast trays for desks and bedside cupboards for storage. Alternatively, create space. All you need is a hallway end, a nook under the stairs or a corner of the living room. The ideal is to establish a dedicated work room where you – or your friends or family – can disappear and remain uninterrupted.

The essentials of any home office are a desk and a chair. High-street stores offer low-priced desks in glass or wood. To save money, buy from office sales, auctions or second-hand office-furniture shops. You don't even need an 'office' desk: an old refectory table, a simple kitchen table, an antique roll-top desk or outdoor dining table will serve the purpose just as well – or make your own by perching a work surface on trestles, bricks or low cupboards.

OPPOSITE **This study occupies part of a living room. In front of the former office desk is an old sewing machinist's chair, which makes a comfortable seat. Other pieces, including the wire tray, the antique fan and the huge old clock, are salvaged from junk shops.**
ABOVE RIGHT **The centrepiece of this work area is a former drawing board, which has been turned into a desk and paired with a tall stool.**
RIGHT AND FAR RIGHT **Storage is always an issue in office spaces. For smaller storage, use everyday containers such as tin cans, jam jars, plastic cups and mugs. For organization on a larger scale, the options include old wooden trunks and box drawers from high-street stationery stores.**

THIS PAGE **A fantastic filing system is shut away behind a plastic sliding door, which helps to preserve light and space. See-through filing boxes are both efficient and economical. Buy them for a snip from high-street stores.**
INSET **In the London home of two artists, the work area flanks a lime-coloured wall. The desk, big enough for both to use at once, is one long bench.**
OPPOSITE **Occupying only an alcove, this home office is a far from stuffy affair. With its hot orange chair, yellow cushion and butter-coloured shelf, this work space is ready for action. All its features – including specialized desk chair and sensible anglepoise lamp – put ergonomics first.**

A work area is often an integral part of a home.

OPPOSITE **This industrial-style home office with its enormous wooden table and metal stools is reminiscent of a genuine workshop. While the ceiling has utility lights for general illumination, a stylish flexible lamp provides adequate task lighting. A galvanized metal floor-to-ceiling cabinet gives plenty of space to stack neatly filed-and-labelled boxes.**
BELOW **A colourful tin can and a homemade wooden block have become pen holders. Good-looking flower heads in a shot glass add panache.**

When it comes to office chairs, it is important to put function before form. To avoid back and neck problems and repetitive strain injury (an inflammation of the wrist joints caused by poor posture), buy an ergonomically designed chair to support your posture. Your feet should be flat on the ground, your wrists at right angles to the desk and your spine straight. You can pick up low-priced office chairs at sales and auctions, but test them out first. Older styles, such as architect's swivel chairs on castors, are office classics and will provide support without making too large a dent in your budget.

Good lighting is another essential. If possible, put your desk under a window so you get plenty of natural light. In the evening, you will need artificial light from a desk lamp, which should be adjustable to provide direct illumination of your work. Most high-street stores have reasonable lights at low prices.

The next thing to consider is accessories. You will need storage and shelving for documents, books, stationery, materials and equipment. For inexpensive shelving, use lengths of bare planks or

ABOVE LEFT **The best things in life are free. This old tin turned wastepaper basket, with its lively design, was found by the roadside.**
ABOVE CENTRE **Home offices do not have to look like conventional offices. In this case, a shower curtain on the table makes a protective desk cover – perfect for creative children as well as adults.**
ABOVE RIGHT **Tiny magnets anchor children's pictures to a cupboard door, softening otherwise steely looks.**

LEFT Any space with a table and chair can be a work zone; this area resembles a sun-filled conservatory.

BELOW LEFT Every desk needs plenty of light, so this long bench desk is perfectly placed. The open space underneath is ideal for storage. Among the numerous options for improvised filing solutions are shopping bags, outsized handbags, wicker picnic baskets and decorated shoeboxes.

OPPOSITE, ABOVE AND BELOW First have breakfast, then set the table for a day's work. A trolley on castors complete with office essentials – a phone, files and printer – is easily moved alongside the desk as needed.

recycled woods, or make use of a bookcase bought from a junk shop. Office sales, auctions and second-hand stores can be wonderful sources of wooden filing cabinets, plain metal drawer units and metal lockers. While distressed paint finishes are appropriate for a rustic, shabby-chic look, for a smarter appearance you can strip back these once-used pieces and revamp them with a fresh coat of paint or varnish.

For office organization on a smaller scale, you can use jam jars, small vases or funky glasses for storing pens, while old leather suitcases, doctor's bags and Perspex plastic drawers (commonly used to hold screws and nails) are ideal for staplers, scissors, rulers, notepads and other accessories. Other boxes, such as re-papered shoe boxes, hat boxes and jewellery chests, make equally chic storage spaces.

As the saying goes, for greater efficiency, you need to 'work smarter, not harder'. When it comes to cheap chic offices, the key is to spend smarter, not harder. After saving what you can on your office set-up, it's time to splash out on that shiny new all-singing, all-dancing personal computer.

top tips for working

DEMARCATE A SPACE For peace of mind, locate your work area away from other activities. Consider whether you can 'reclaim' a room from a hallway or under the stairs, where you can shut the door on work at the end of the day.

GIVE PRIORITY TO BASICS If you don't have a whole room to dedicate to a work space, try a corner of a room, or use your kitchen table, but build in adequate storage nearby.

DOUBLE UP Alternatively, install a fold-out desk in a convenient corner. All you need is a solid piece of painted MDF on hinges that can be hidden away in a cupboard when not required. Freestanding units are available from high-street stores, or you can have your own built by a carpenter.

CREATE A LOOK Go retro or Bohemian chic, for example. Team a weathered kitchen table with an old architect's swivel chair and accessorize with storage boxes covered in floral wallpaper.

THINK ERGONOMIC When it comes to desk and chairs, spend wisely, with your health in mind. It's easy to create a desk – but office chairs have been specially designed to give good back support.

sources

GENERAL

B&Q
0845 222 1000 for stores
www.diy.com
*Excellent DIY store. Bargains
include tiles, flooring and basic
white bathroom furniture.*

Habitat
196 Tottenham Court Road
London W1T 7LG
0845 601 0740 for stores
www.habitat.net
*Everything for the modern home,
including plain and trendy tablewares,
bedding; kitchen and bathroom
accessories; and re-runs of classic
modern designs.*

Homebase
0870 900 8098 for stores
www.homebase.co.uk
*Basic well-sourced home and garden
superstore. Inexpensive laminate
flooring, outdoor furniture and
bathroom fittings. Good-value paints.*

IKEA
020 8208 5600
www.ikea.co.uk
*Fabulous centre for home and outdoor
products. Well-priced bathrooms and
kitchens. Bargain fabrics and window
treatments, along with rugs, laminate
flooring, modern white ceramics,
cutlery and lighting.*

John Lewis
020 7629 7711 for stores and
information
www.johnlewis.com
*Department stores with everything for
the home: quality kitchen basics,
fabrics, paints, bedding and flooring;
plus a good stock of traditional blue-
and-white-striped cornishware.*

PAINTS & DECORATIVE FINISHES

Auro Organic Paint Supplies
01799 543 077
www.auroorganic.co.uk
*Natural emulsion, eggshell and chalk
paints in a range of muted colours.
Also floor finishes and wood stains.*

Crown Decorative Products
0870 240 1127 for stockists
and information.
www.crownpaint.co.uk
*Pioneer of odour-free and one-coat
paints. Specializes in up-to-date
colours and finishes. Ranges include
textured paint and shimmer effects.*

Designers Guild
267–271 & 275–277 King's Road
London SW3 5EN
020 7351 5775 for store
020 7243 7300 for stockists
and mail order
www.designersguild.com
*Contemporary paint colours in matt
emulsion and water-based eggshell.
Inspiring fabrics and wallpapers, too.*

Dulux
01753 550 555 for stockists,
advice and product information
www.dulux.co.uk
*Vast range of paint colours and finishes,
plus a reliable colour-matching service.
Visit the website and try before you
buy with the virtual mousepainter.*

Farrow & Ball
01202 876 141 for stockists, advice
and product information
www.farrow-ball.co.uk
*Good range of old-fashioned matt
colours originally created for The
National Trust. Excellent selection
of off-whites.*

International Paints
01962 717 001 for stockists, advice
and product information
www.international-paints.co.uk
*High-quality paints for a range of
decorating problems, ranging from
anti-damp paint to special decorative
finishes such as tile gloss.*

Plasti-Kote
01223 836400 for stockists
www.spraypaint.co.uk
*Easy-to-apply decorative finishes and
flat colour; allow you to revamp second-
hand white goods in an instant.*

The Stencil Library
01661 844 844 for information and
catalogue
www.stencil-library.com
*Online catalogue of over 3,500 stencil
designs. Paints and varnishes for
fabrics, furniture and walls.*

FABRICS

Cath Kidston
8 Clarendon Cross
London W11
020 7221 4248 for stores and
stockists
020 7221 8000 for mail order
www.cathkidston.co.uk
*Bright and fresh 1950s-inspired florals
and accessories. Fabrics available by
the metre.*

The Cloth Shop
290 Portobello Road
London W10 5TE
020 8986 6001
*Well-priced natural fibres; everything
from winter wools to summery stripes,
sari silks and antique linen.*

Ian Mankin
109 Regents Park Road
London NW1 8UR
020 7722 0997 for store and
mail order
*Excellent stock of utility fabrics, ticking,
checks and stripes. Also gingham, plain
cotton and linen.*

MacCulloch & Wallis
25 Dering Street
London W1R 0BH
020 7629 0311 for store and
mail order
www.macculloch-wallis.co.uk
*Great range of fabrics and trimmings,
including bright silks (to decorate
windows), mohair (to make blankets)
and feather trimmings (to add to a
dull lampshade).*

Malabar
Unit 31-33
The Southbank Business Centre
Ponton Road
London SW8 5BL
020 7501 4200 for stockists
www.malabar.co.uk
*Fantastic fabric range including
inexpensive hand-loomed cottons
and sumptuous silks.*

Marimekko
16–17 St Christopher's Place
London W1U 1NZ
020 7486 6454 for store and
information
www.marimekko.co.uk
*Finnish-designed bags, clothes,
kitchen and bathroom accessories.
Bright, dramatically patterned
fabrics sold by the metre.*

FLOORING

The Alternative Flooring Company
01264 335111 for stockists
www.alternative-flooring.co.uk
*Natural flooring products made of
100 per cent natural fibres from
renewable sources: seagrass, coir,
sisal, jute and wool.*

Dalsouple
01984 667 233 for stockists
www.dalsouple.com
*Textured and smooth rubber floor
tiles in a wide range of colours.*

The Flokati Rug Company
Unit C, 11b Wier Road
London SW12 0LT
020 8675 2442 for information
and mail order
www.flokatirugco.co.uk
*Widest range in UK of 100 per cent
pure wool flokati rugs; naturally
waterproof, they make great bath
mats. Also Greek kilims.*

Natural Flooring Direct
0800 454 721 for information
and brochure
www.naturalflooringdirect.com
*Natural flooring from sustainable
sources. Also good for unusual
materials such as bamboo and paper.*

Siesta Cork Tile Co.
020 8683 4055 for information
www.siestacorktiles.co.uk
Suppliers of matt, satin or colour tinted cork tiles. Also cork rolls for notice boards and cork veneer wallpaper.

STORAGE

The Holding Company
241–245 Kings Road
London SW3 5EL
020 7352 1600 for store
020 8445 2888 for mail order
www.theholdingcompany.com
Storage with style in the shape of leather chests, perspex and mesh organizers, mobile shelves, zinc furniture and chrome racking.

Lakeland Limited
01539 488 300 for branches
and mail order
www.lakelandlimited.com
Great for all sorts of storage solutions, including cheap plastic storage boxes.

Muji
6-17 Tottenham Court Road
London W1P 9DP
020 7323 2208 for information
www.muji.co.uk
Practical and stylish household and fashion items from Japan. Particularly good for basic storage needs, small and large.

FURNITURE & ACCESSORIES

After Noah
121 Upper Street
London N1 1QP
020 7359 4281 for information
www.afternoah.com
Eclectic mix of contemporary and vintage furniture and homewares

Baileys Home & Garden
The Engine Shed, Station Approach
Ross-on-Wye
Herefordshire HR9 7BW
01989 563015
sales@baileys-home-garden.co.uk
www.baileyshomeandgarden.com
Wide range of home accessories. Mail order.

The Bigger Picture
020 7636 9000
www.mybiggerpicture.com
Transform your photographs into cushions, bags, huge canvases or even wallpaper. Images can also be converted to sepia or black and white.

Britart
60–62 Commercial Street
London E1 6LT
020 7392 7200
www.britart.com
Original and contemporary art, photographs and prints.

Creative Beadcraft
01494 715 606 for catalogue
and mail order
www.creativebeadcraft.co.uk
A good selection of beads in every style, plus all those inspiring extras – sequins, trimmings, and so on.

Emily Readett Bayley
01400 281 563 for stockists
www.emilyreadettbayley.com
A British designer working with Asian craftspeople and sustainable materials to produce an eclectic mix of homewares.

Inexterior
020 7739 2026 for information
www.inexterior.co.uk
Leather cubes, cushions and beanbags, and bohemian animal-skin rugs, all at great prices. Private commissions undertaken in an amazing choice of colours and styles.

J.W. Bollom & Co
020 8658 2299
www.bollom.com
Great range of felt; perfect for home-made rugs and innovative placemats.

Lombok
555 Kings Road
London SW6 2EB
020 7736 0001
www.lombox.co.uk
Fantastic collection of affordable reclaimed teak furniture alongside original Javanese accessories. Good for large statement pieces.

Monsoon Home
33c Kings Road
London SW3 4LY
020 7313 3000
www.monsoon.co.uk
Inspirational decorative pieces to adorn the home.

Pol's Potten
www.polspotten.nl
Furniture, lighting, accessories including terracotta and glass, and custom-made kitchens.

Prices Candles
020 7228 3345 for stockists
www.prices-candles.co.uk
Leading candle manufacturer and distributor in the UK.

Voodoo Blue
020 8560 7050 for stockists and
mail order
www.voodooblue.co.uk
Fair-traded hand-woven sisal and soapstone products from Kenya, plus a fantastic range of melamine tableware.

www.oceanuk.com
Good-value modern furniture and accessories available online.

KITCHEN & BATHROOM SPECIALISTS

Builders Iron & Zincwork
020 8443 3300 for information
Suppliers of zinc and stainless-steel sheets. They will cut pieces to size and make up worktops.

Buyers and Sellers
120 Ladbroke Grove
London W1 5NE
0845 085 5585
American refrigerators; stainless-steel and coloured appliances.

David Mellor
4 Sloane Square
London SW1W 8EE
020 7730 4259
www.davidmellordesign.co.uk
Specialists in cutlery and fine kitchenware. Good source of quality kitchen basics.

GEC Anderson
01442 826 999 for information
www.gecanderson.co.uk
Stainless-steel kitchen and bathroom pieces.

Ideal Standard
01482 346 461 for stockists
www.idealstandard.co.uk
Plain and functional baths, lavatories and other bathroom fixtures.

Pages
121 Shaftesbury Avenue
London WC2H 8AD
020 7565 5934
for information
www.pagescatering.co.uk
Catering equipment including basic industrial ovens, trolleys, pots and pans.

Twyfords
0870 020 0099 for showrooms
www.twyfordbathrooms.com
Bathroom fittings and furnishings in simple shapes and with clean lines.

SECOND-HAND & ANTIQUES

For used and antique items that you can reuse and recycle, visit street markets and car-boot sales and scour local junk and second-hand shops. A selection of other resources are listed below.

Lassco House & Garden
St Michael's Church
Mark Street
London EC2A 4ER
020 7749 9944
www.lassco.co.uk
Architectural antiques and salvage, including reclaimed wooden panelling and flooring.

www.salvoweb.com
A wonderful source of antique, reclaimed, salvaged, recycled and reproduction items.

www.ebay.com
Internet auctions; every category of merchandize represented.

picture credits

All photography by Debi Treloar unless otherwise stated.

Key: a=above, b=below, r=right, l=left, c=centre.

Endpapers Anna Massee of Het Grote Avontuur (The Great Adventure)'s home in Amsterdam; **1** Debi Treloar's family home in north-west London; **2** The home of Patty Collister in London, owner of An Angel At My Table; **3l** Susan Cropper's family home in London, www.63hlg.com; **4** Sue Withers & Andrew Moller's apartment in London, designed by Dive Architects; **5** Mark Chalmers' apartment in Amsterdam. Kitchen custom-made by Pol's Potten; **6a** Cristine Tholstrup Hermansen and Helge Drenck's house in Copenhagen; **6b & 6–7** Debi Treloar's family home in north-west London; **7r** The home of Patty Collister in London, owner of An Angel At My Table; **8al** Clare and David Mannix-Andrews' house, Hove, East Sussex; **8ar** A London apartment designed by James Soane and Christopher Ash of Project Orange; **8b** Artist David Hopkins' house in East London, designed by Yen-Yen Teh of Emulsion; **9–10** Mark and Sally of Baileys Home and Garden's house in Herefordshire; **11** Annelie Bruijn's home in Amsterdam; **12–13** Debi Treloar's family home in north-west London; **14** Susan Cropper's family home in London, www.63hlg.com; **15l & r** Dominique Coughlin's apartment in London; **15c** Mark and Sally of Baileys Home and Garden's house in Herefordshire; **16a** Anna Massee of Het Grote Avontuur (The Great Adventure)'s home in Amsterdam; **16b** The home of Studio Aandacht. Design by Ben Lambers; **16–17** Sue Withers & Andrew Moller's apartment in London, designed by Dive Architects; **17r** North London flat of presentation skills trainer/actress and her teacher husband, designed by Gordana Mandic of Buildburo; **18** The home of Studio Aandacht. Design by Ben Lambers; **19l** Annelie Bruijn's home in Amsterdam; **19r** Anna Massee of Het Grote Avontuur (The Great Adventure)'s home in Amsterdam; **20al** The home of Patty Collister in London, owner of An Angel At My Table; **20ar** Dominique Coughlin's apartment in London; **20bl & 21** Clare and David Mannix-Andrews' house, Hove, East Sussex; **22al** Mark Chalmers' apartment in Amsterdam; **22ar** The home of Studio Aandacht. Design by Ben Lambers; **22bl** The designer couple Tea Bendix & Tobias Jacobsen's home, Denmark; **22br & 23** Mark and Sally of Baileys Home and Garden's house in Herefordshire; **24l & 25 inset** The home of Patty Collister in London, owner of An Angel At My Table; **26l & ar** Anna Massee of Het Grote Avontuur (The Great Adventure)'s home in Amsterdam; **26br** Annelie Bruijn's home in Amsterdam; **27** Cristine Tholstrup Hermansen and Helge Drenck's house in Copenhagen; **28 & 29ar** Susan Cropper's family home in London, www.63hlg.com; **29al** Annelie Bruijn's home in Amsterdam; **29bl** Debi Treloar's family home in north-west London; **29br** Morag Myerscough's house in Clerkenwell, London – her house gallery/shop; **30–31** Susan Cropper's family home in London, www.63hlg.com; **31l** Wim and Josephine's apartment in Amsterdam; **31r** The home of Studio Aandacht. Design by Ben Lambers; **32l & a** Mark and Sally of Baileys Home and Garden's house in Herefordshire; **32br** Clare and David Mannix-Andrews' house, Hove, East Sussex; **33** Annelie Bruijn's home in Amsterdam; **34al** Nicky Phillips' apartment in London; **34bl** Debi Treloar's family home in north-west London; **34r–35** The home of Patty Collister in London, owner of An Angel At My Table; **36a** Susan Cropper's family home in London, www.63hlg.com; **36b** Cristine Tholstrup Hermansen and Helge Drenck's house in Copenhagen; **37** Mark and Sally of Baileys Home and Garden's house in Herefordshire; **38–39** Artist David Hopkins' house in East London, designed by Yen-Yen Teh of Emulsion; **39r** Morag Myerscough's house in Clerkenwell, London – her house gallery/shop, photograph by Richard Learoyd; **40** Clare and David Mannix-Andrews' house, Hove, East Sussex; **41a** Annelie Bruijn's home in Amsterdam; **41bl** Cristine Tholstrup Hermansen and Helge Drenck's house in Copenhagen; **41bc** Anna Massee of Het Grote Avontuur (The Great Adventure)'s home in Amsterdam; **41br** Wim and Josephine's apartment in Amsterdam; **42** The designer couple Tea Bendix & Tobias Jacobsen's home, Denmark; **43l** Mark and Sally of Baileys Home and Garden's house in Herefordshire; **43r** Nicky Phillips' apartment in London; **44al** Clare and David Mannix-Andrews' house, Hove, East Sussex; **44ar** Mark and Sally of Baileys Home and Garden's house in Herefordshire; **44b** Sue Withers & Andrew Moller's apartment in London, designed by Dive Architects; **45** Nicky Phillips' apartment in London; **46** Mark and Sally of Baileys Home and Garden's house in Herefordshire; **47l** The home of Patty Collister in London, owner of An Angel At My Table; **47r** Clare and David Mannix-Andrews' house, Hove, East Sussex; **48l** Cristine Tholstrup Hermansen and Helge Drenck's house in Copenhagen; **48–49** The home of Patty Collister in London, owner of An Angel At My Table; **49br** Nicky Phillips' apartment in London; **50** Sue Withers & Andrew Moller's apartment in London, designed by Dive Architects; **51** Wim and Josephine's apartment in Amsterdam; **52l** Morag Myerscough's house in Clerkenwell, London – her house gallery/shop; **52c** Mark and Sally of Baileys Home and Garden's house in Herefordshire; **52r** The designer couple Tea Bendix & Tobias Jacobsen's home, Denmark; **53** Sue Withers & Andrew Moller's apartment in London, designed by Dive Architects; **54l** Wim and Josephine's apartment in Amsterdam; **54–55** Mark and Sally of Baileys Home and Garden's house in Herefordshire; **56–57** Anna Massee of Het Grote Avontuur (The Great Adventure)'s home in Amsterdam; **58 & 59r** Annelie Bruijn's home in Amsterdam; **59l & c** Anna Massee of Het Grote Avontuur (The Great Adventure)'s home in Amsterdam; **60** The home of Patty Collister in London, owner of An Angel At My Table; **60–61** Mark Chalmers' apartment in Amsterdam; **61r** The home of Studio Aandacht. Design by Ben Lambers; **63al** Artist David Hopkins' house in East London, designed by Yen-Yen Teh of Emulsion; **63r** Mark and Sally of Baileys Home and Garden's house in Herefordshire; **64al** Cristine Tholstrup Hermansen and Helge Drenck's house in Copenhagen; **64b** Anna Massee of Het Grote Avontuur (The Great Adventure)'s home in Amsterdam; **65** Wim and Josephine's apartment in Amsterdam; **66l & ar** Mark Chalmers' apartment in Amsterdam; **66cr** Artist David Hopkins' house in East London, designed by Yen-Yen Teh of Emulsion; **66br & 67** Wim and Josephine's apartment in Amsterdam; **67 inset** Mark and Sally of Baileys Home and Garden's house in Herefordshire; **68a** Mark Chalmers' apartment in Amsterdam; **68bl** Debi Treloar's family home in north-west London; **68br** Anna Massee of Het Grote Avontuur (The Great Adventure)'s home in Amsterdam; **68r** Annelie Bruijn's home in Amsterdam; **69** Susan Cropper's family home in London, www.63hlg.com; **70l** Mark Chalmers' apartment in Amsterdam; **70r** Mark and Sally of Baileys Home and Garden's house in Herefordshire; **71** Wim and Josephine's apartment in Amsterdam; **72al** Dominique Coughlin's apartment in London; **72bl** Susan Cropper's family home in London, www.63hlg.com; **72r–73** Sue Withers & Andrew Moller's apartment in London, designed by Dive Architects; **74a** Susan Cropper's family home in London, www.63hlg.com; **74bl** Sue Withers & Andrew Moller's apartment in London, designed by Dive Architects; **74bc & r** Nicky Phillips' apartment in London; **75** Mark Chalmers' apartment in Amsterdam; **75 inset** Susan Cropper's family home in London, www.63hlg.com; **76** Mark and Sally of Baileys Home and Garden's house in Herefordshire; **77al** Clare and David Mannix-Andrews' house, Hove, East Sussex; **77ar & bl** A London apartment designed by James Soane and Christopher Ash of Project Orange; **77br** Susan Cropper's family home in London, www.63hlg.com; **78** Sue Withers & Andrew Moller's apartment in London, designed by Dive Architects; **79al** Mark and Sally of Baileys Home and Garden's house in Herefordshire; **79bl** Mark Chalmers' apartment in Amsterdam; **79r–80l** Artist David Hopkins' house in East London, designed by Yen-Yen Teh of Emulsion; **80c** Anna Massee of Het Grote Avontuur (The Great Adventure)'s home in Amsterdam; **80–81** Susan Cropper's family home in London, www.63hlg.com; **81c** North London flat of presentation skills trainer/actress and her teacher husband, designed by Gordana Mandic of Buildburo; **81r–82l** Artist David Hopkins' house in East London, designed by Yen-Yen Teh of Emulsion; **82ar** Debi Treloar's family home in north-west London; **82br** The home of Studio Aandacht. Design by Ben Lambers; **83** Mark and Sally of Baileys Home and Garden's house in Herefordshire; **84** A London apartment designed by James Soane and Christopher Ash of Project Orange; **84–85** Mark Chalmers' apartment in Amsterdam; **86** Nicky Phillips' apartment in London; **87a** A London apartment designed by James Soane and Christopher Ash of Project Orange; **87b & 88–89** Mark and Sally of Baileys Home and Garden's house in Herefordshire; **89ar** Morag Myerscough's house in Clerkenwell, London – her house gallery/shop. Graffiti painting by Luke Morgan; **89br** Artist David Hopkins' house in East London, designed by Yen-Yen Teh of Emulsion; **90–91a** Cristine Tholstrup Hermansen and Helge Drenck's house in Copenhagen; **91b**

Annelie Bruijn's home in Amsterdam; **92–93** The home of Studio Aandacht. Design by Ben Lambers; **94–95** Anna Massee of Het Grote Avontuur (The Great Adventure)'s home in Amsterdam; **96l & 97b** Annelie Bruijn's home in Amsterdam. Wall spray stencil of deer's head by Barnaby Irish; **96–97 & 97a** Debi Treloar's family home in north-west London; **98–99a** Mark Chalmers' apartment in Amsterdam. Kitchen custom-made by Pol's Potten; **99b** Artist David Hopkins' house in East London, designed by Yen-Yen Teh of Emulsion; **100l** The home of Studio Aandacht. Design by Ben Lambers; **100–101** The designer couple Tea Bendix & Tobias Jacobsen's home, Denmark; **102** Sue Withers & Andrew Moller's apartment in London, designed by Dive Architects; **103** Nicky Phillips' apartment in London; **104b–105** Cristine Tholstrup Hermansen and Helge Drenck's house in Copenhagen; **106 & 107r** Anna Massee of Het Grote Avontuur (The Great Adventure)'s home in Amsterdam; **107l & c** Debi Treloar's family home in north-west London; **108l** Clare and David Mannix-Andrews' house, Hove, East Sussex; **108–109** Nicky Phillips' apartment in London; **109r** Susan Cropper's family home in London, www.63hlg.com; **110 & 111r** The designer couple Tea Bendix & Tobias Jacobsen's home, Denmark; **111l** Mark and Sally of Baileys Home and Garden's house in Herefordshire; **112–113** Cristine Tholstrup Hermansen and Helge Drenck's house in Copenhagen; **114 & 115br** Clare and David Mannix-Andrews' house, Hove, East Sussex; **115a, bl & c** Wim and Josephine's apartment in Amsterdam; **116–117** Clare and David Mannix-Andrews' house, Hove, East Sussex; **117 inset** Wim and Josephine's apartment in Amsterdam; **118a–119** Susan Cropper's family home in London, www.63hlg.com; **120l & 121ar** Morag Myerscough's house in Clerkenwell, London – her house gallery/shop; **120–121 & 121b** Annelie Bruijn's home in Amsterdam; **122–123l** Clare and David Mannix-Andrews' house, Hove, East Sussex; **123r** A London apartment designed by James Soane and Christopher Ash of Project Orange; **124–125a** Susan Cropper's family home in London, www.63hlg.com; **125b** The home of Patty Collister in London, owner of An Angel At My Table; **126l** Artist David Hopkins' house in East London, designed by Yen-Yen Teh of Emulsion; **126r–127** Mark and Sally of Baileys Home and Garden's house in Herefordshire; **128** Morag Myerscough's house in Clerkenwell, London – her house gallery/shop, photograph by Richard Learoyd; **129** Debi Treloar's family home in north-west London; **130l & c** Susan Cropper's family home in London, www.63hlg.com; **130–131** Nicky Phillips' apartment in London; **132** Mark and Sally of Baileys Home and Garden's house in Herefordshire; **133** Clare and David Mannix-Andrews' house, Hove, East Sussex; **134** North London flat of presentation skills trainer/actress and her teacher husband, designed by Gordana Mandic of Buildburo; **135** Sue Withers & Andrew Moller's apartment in London, designed by Dive Architects; **136–137** Wim and Josephine's apartment in Amsterdam; **138a** The home of Studio Aandacht. Design by Ben Lambers; **138b** Cristine Tholstrup Hermansen and Helge Drenck's house in Copenhagen; **138–139** Sue Withers & Andrew Moller's apartment in London, designed by Dive Architects; **139r** Dominique Coughlin's apartment in London.

business credits

An Angel At My Table
116A Fortess Road
London NW5 2HL
020 7424 9777
and
14 High Street
Saffron Walden
Essex CB10 1AY
01799 528777
Painted furniture and accessories.
Pages 2, 7r, 20al, 24l, 25 inset, 34r, 35, 47l, 48-49, 60, 125b.

Annelie Bruijn
+ 31 653 702869
annelie_bruijn@email.com
Pages 11, 19l, 26br, 29al, 33, 41a, 58, 59r, 68r, 91b, 96l, 97b, 120–121, 121b.

Archie Cunningham Furniture and Interior Solutions
020 8674 1743
www.archiecunningham.com
Pages 15l & r, 20ar, 72al, 139r.

Baileys Home & Garden
The Engine Shed
Station Approach
Ross-on-Wye
Herefordshire HR9 7BW
01989 563015
sales@baileys-home-garden.co.uk
www.baileyshomeandgarden.com
Pages 9, 10, 15c, 23, 32l & a, 37, 43l, 44ar, 46, 52c, 54r–55, 63r, 67 inset, 70r, 76, 79al, 83, 87b, 88–89, 111l, 126r, 127, 132.

buildburo ltd
7 Tetcott Road
London SW10 OSA
020 7352 1092
www.buildburo.co.uk
Pages 17r, 81c, 134.

DIVE Architects
10 Park Street
London SE1 9AB
020 7407 0955
mail@divearchitects.com
www.divearchitects.com
Pages 4, 16–17, 44b, 50, 53, 72r–73, 74bl, 78, 102, 135, 138–139.

Emulsion
172 Foundling Court
Brunswick Centre
London WC1N 1QE
020 7833 4533
contact@emulsionarchitecture.com
www.emulsionarchitecture.com
Pages 8b, 38–39, 63al, 66cr, 79r–80l, 81r–82l, 89br, 99b, 126l.

her house
30d Great Sutton Street
London EC1V ODS
020 7689 0606/0808
morag@herhouse.uk.com
www.herhouse.uk.com
Pages 29br, 39r, 52l, 89ar, 120l, 121ar, 128.

Het Grote Avontuur
Haarlemmerstraat 25
1013 JE Amsterdam
The Netherlands
www.hetgroteavontuur.nl
+ 31 20 6268597
and
Het Grote Avontuur Deel 2
Visseringstraat 31
1051 KH Amsterdam
The Netherlands
www.hetgroteavontuur.nl
Pages endpapers, 16a, 19r, 26l & ar, 41bc, 56–57, 59l & c, 64b, 68br, 80c, 94–95, 106–107r.

Josephine Macrander
Interior Designer
+ 31 299 402804
Pages 31l, 41br, 51, 54l, 65, 66br, 67, 71, 115a, bl & c, 117 inset, 136–37.

Project Orange
1st Floor Morelands
7 Old Street
London EC1V 9HL
020 7689 3456
www.projectorange.com
Pages 8ar, 77ar & bl, 84, 87a, 123r.

SAD Interiors
07930 626916
sad@flymedia.co.uk
Pages 8b, 38-39, 63al, 66cr, 79r–80l, 81r–82l, 89br, 99b, 126l.

Susan Cropper
www.63hlg.com
Pages 3l, 14, 28, 29ar, 30–31, 36a, 69, 72bl, 74a, 75 inset, 77br, 80-81, 109r, 118a–119, 124–125a, 130l & c.

Studio Aandacht
Art Direction and Interior Production
ben.lambers@studioaandacht.nl
www.studioaandacht.nl
Pages 16b, 18, 22ar, 31r, 61r, 82br, 92, 93, 100l, 138a.

Tobias Jacobsen & Tea Bendix
www.tobiasjacobsen.dk
Pages 22bl, 42, 52r, 100–101, 110, 111r.

with thanks to:
Echo Design Agency
5 Sebastian Street
London EC1V OHD
020 7251 6990
enquiry@echodesign.co.uk
A directory of architects and designers.
Pages 8b, 38-39, 63al, 66cr, 79r–80l, 81r–82l, 89br, 99b, 126l.

index

acknowledgments

Emily Chalmers would like to thank all the owners who let us into their stylish and inspiring homes. Thanks also to Debi, the best photographer and friend, who is a joy to work with. Thank you to Gabriella and Alison at Ryland Peters & Small for giving me another great opportunity and the chance to meet Ali, a gifted wordster and fab new mother; and to Catherine and Henrietta, who put it all together.

Ali Hanan would like to thank the lovely Claire Hector for introducing me to Ryland Peters & Small, Henrietta Heald for her sensitive, eloquent editing, Alison Starling for the opportunity, and Emily Chalmers for her inspiration. I also thank my parents, the Dame and Murray Hanan, and my partner, Dizzy, for looking after our son Luca, who was born halfway through the long birth of this book.